CELEBRATION SERIES®

THE PIANO ODYSSEY®

STUDENT
WORKBOOK

8

A Note to Students

Congratulations!

You are about to embark on an exciting musical journey!

For each piece of music you study in the *Celebration Series®*, Levels 1 through 8, you will be able to work through the exercises, games, and creative activities chosen by the authors for that particular piece. Since the authors are all teachers at The Royal Conservatory of Music in Toronto, Canada, you can be sure you are receiving the best advice on how to learn your chosen repertoire.

Always remember that you need to use this *Workbook* alongside your *Piano Repertoire* album. Fill in the blanks, think about and answer the questions, and have fun with the activities. It is also a great idea to listen to the recording of your piece as a model of how it should be played once you have learned it well.

Musical terms you may need help with are printed in **bold type**. These terms are defined in the Glossary at the back of the *Workbook*. This Glossary is meant as a quick reference only. For more detailed information about theory, please refer to theory textbook materials such as Grace Vandendool's *Keyboard Theory Series*, or Mark Sarnecki's *Elementary Music Rudiments*, both published by The Frederick Harris Music Company. If you want a quick reference for where your favorite composers fit into musical history, check the side margin of each page.

Most of all, remember that learning to play the piano well and discovering wonderful repertoire from many style periods — Baroque, Classical, Romantic, and 20th century — will prepare you for a lifelong love and enjoyment of music.

A Note to Teachers

At all times in their study, students should feel the excitement of embarking on a musical journey. The subtitle of the *Celebration Series®* — *The Piano Odyssey®* — is meant to evoke something of this spirit.

In working through this interactive *Student Workbook*, piano students are led to discover the essence of each piece they study, whether it be from the Baroque, Classical, Romantic, or 20th-century repertoire. Each era has unlimited potential for students who are truly engaged by a thoughtful and thought-provoking presentation of the material. Thus, teachers are encouraged to utilize the full spectrum of materials encompassed in the *Celebration Series®* library, from *Piano Repertoire* and *Piano Studies/Etudes* albums, through recordings and these *Student Workbooks*, in order to lead students from the printed page through the listening experience to the physical realization of the work in performance. In addition, the *Celebration Series® Handbook for Teachers* is an indispensable companion to the *Student Workbooks*, as well as a comprehensive guide to studying and teaching the entire body of works encompassed in Levels 1 through 10 of the *Celebration Series®, The Piano Odyssey®*.

Cover and book designers: FiWired.com
Music engraver: Simon Jutras

National Library of Canada cataloguing in publication data

Main entry under title:

Celebration series : the piano odyssey : student workbook

(Celebration series)
To be used with the Piano repertoire album.
First ed. published under title: Piano study guide series; previous ed. published under title: Student guide.

ISBN 0-88797-738-3 (v. 8)

1. Piano – Instruction and study. I. Royal Conservatory of Music. II. Title: Piano repertoire album. III. Title: Piano odyssey. IV. Title: Student guide. V. Series.

MT245.P583 2001 786.2'07 C00-933325-8

Contents

Little Prelude in E Minor, BWV 938
Little Prelude in D Major, BWV 936

Johann Sebastian Bach (1685–1750)

Piano Repertoire 8
page 4

CD 8 / tracks 1 & 2

In 1717, Bach accepted an offer from Prince Leopold of Anhalt-Cöthen to serve as *Kappellmeister*. The Prince was a talented musician who loved and understood music. During his five years at Cöthen, Bach wrote mainly instrumental music — suites, concertos, sonatas, and keyboard music. The *Brandenburg Concertos* and the first book of the *Well-Tempered Clavier* date from this period.

Bach was an outstanding performer on keyboard instruments and especially esteemed as an organist. He was often hired to play on newly-constructed instruments and to comment on their quality, travelling far from his home to do so. Bach was also one of the great teachers of the Baroque era. He had many students, and he also taught music to his children; four of them became well-known composers. Bach's students often lived in his household and helped him with various musical tasks.

Little Preludes

Among the wide variety of pieces Bach wrote for teaching purposes are about 18 short preludes. These "little preludes" were intended to show students how to elaborate on chord sequences and how to build a **contrapuntal** structure around a single distinctive motive. As a teacher, Bach emphasized "a clear, clean touch of all the fingers of both hands," and the little preludes provide excellent practice for this. Their linear structure calls for a firm, even touch for each note. The little preludes also lay the foundation for the more advanced contrapuntal writing in Bach's Inventions, Sinfonias, and the *Well-Tempered Clavier*.

There are a number of short preludes in the *Wilhelm Friedemann Bach Notebook*, but the two little preludes included in *Piano Repertoire 8* are from a set probably written during Bach's time at Cöthen, entitled *Six Small Preludes for Beginners on the Clavier*, BWV 933–938.

According to Baroque Musicians. . .

We are fortunate to have descriptions of acceptable performance practice written by musicians of Bach's day. These 18th-century writers describe a *legato* touch for *cantabile* melodies and a non-*legato* touch for lively, faster passages.

> Different from *legato* and *staccato* is the ordinary movement which consists of lifting the finger from the last key shortly before touching the next note. This ordinary movement, which is always understood, is never indicated.
>
> (F.W. Marpurg, *Guide to Keyboard Playing*, Berlin, 1755)

> The briskness of *allegros* is conveyed by detached notes . . . There are many who perform stickily, as if they had glue between their fingers. They hold notes too long. Others, trying to correct this, leave the keys too soon, as if they were red-hot. Both [approaches] are incorrect. Midway between these extremes is best.
>
> (C.P.E. Bach, *Essay on the True Art of Playing Keyboard Instruments*, Berlin, 1753)

What is a Prelude?

In the Baroque era, a prelude was simply a piece of music that came before another piece of music — such as a fugue or a suite of dance movements. These pieces were intended to catch the listener's attention and prepare them for the more important, more serious, or more complicated music that was to follow, and to establish the key. Preludes have a free form and an **improvisatory** style. Sometimes they were actually improvised. Most preludes consist of repeated figures based on broken chords or scale passages. They provided an excellent opportunity to try out the keyboard of the instrument and test the acoustics of the room. Many preludes combine rhythmical sections with passages in a freer rhythmic style.

Counterpoint

The literal meaning of the term **counterpoint** is "point against point" — or note against note. Music that is written in a contrapuntal style consists of two or more independent lines, or voices. Both the E minor and the D major preludes have a contrapuntal texture, and both are characterized by a constant forward motion best described by the German term *Fortspinnung*. The music is spun out in an uninterrupted line toward the **cadence** at the end of a section.

Little Prelude in E Minor, BWV 938

This prelude is the last of Bach's *Six Small Preludes for Beginners*, and is probably the most challenging to play. Bach uses two different contrapuntal techniques in this prelude: **imitation** and **sequence**.

Form

The double bar lines and repeat signs divide this prelude into two sections, indicating binary form.

Are both sections the same length? yes

Are the two sections similar in character or do they present a contrast?

They present contrast.

Label the two sections with letters in your score, and add the letters and measure numbers to this form chart.

A	mm. 1 – 20	closing key: B+
B	mm. 21 – 48	closing key: e –

Play mm. 1–20 slowly, and listen particularly for **modulations**. (You may find it easier to play only the essential notes in mm. 9–20 and listen to the **implied harmony**.) Now play mm. 20–48. Add the closing keys to the form chart.

Imitation

The musical material in mm. 1–4 is deceptively simple.

Name the chord outlined by the RH in mm. 1–2. e –

How does Bach create contrast within this short motive?

By changing key.

Does the LH play an exact imitation of this motive? If not, what is different?

Yes.

Name the chord outlined by the RH in mm. 3–4. B+

Is this second RH statement an exact imitation of the first?

No.

What is the key in these measures, and how does it relate to the home key?

First e⁻, then B+. e⁻ is the home key and B+ is the dominant 7th.

Is the motive transposed exactly? yes except for one note.

Where does Bach present a similar pattern of imitation using the same motive?

in mm 21-24.

Name the chords outlined in these measures.

B9 , E9

The main motive of this prelude is an excellent example of the fact that counterpoint and harmony are inseparable. Although counterpoint is linear, harmony is implied both by the combination of voices, and by the chords outlined by each single voice.

Sequences

The sequences in this prelude serve two purposes.

1. They continue the musical line by repeating a pattern at different intervals.
2. They repeat harmonic references, such as broken-chord patterns.

Play mm. 5–8, then take a close look at the music.

What is the interval difference between mm. 5 and 7?

+ 2nd.

Now look at the harmonic content of mm. 6 and 8. What do you hear in each case?

a-7 G7

Suspensions

In the second section, there are a number of notes tied over the bar line. Some of these notes fit into the harmony of both measures. Others are **suspensions** — they fit the harmony of the first measure but have been held over, creating a temporary **dissonance**.

Find two examples of each type.

notes that fit with both measures: 1. Bar 25-26
2. 26-27

suspensions: 1. Bar 22-23
2. 46-47.

Ornamentation

Ornamentation plays a significant role in Baroque music.

How would you describe the effect of the ornaments in this prelude?

____

This piece has a number of LH **mordents**. Have you played any other pieces that have a similar pattern of ornamentation?

No.

____

Little Prelude in D Major, BWV 936

Contrapuntal Tricks

How many voices are there in this prelude? ___________

Are all the voices active all the way through? ___________

Which voice drops out, and where does this happen?

____

Which voice might be described as a walking bass? ___________

This regular rhythm creates a gentle pulse that grounds the other voices. The contrapuntal interplay of the upper voices displays three techniques used by Baroque composers:

1. imitation
2. inversion (the voices trade places)
3. sequence

Here are three excerpts from Bach's D major prelude. Find them in your score, play them (along with the adjoining measures), then write the measure numbers and the correct technique label above the excerpt.

Excerpt A mm. _____ ____________________

Excerpt B mm. _____ ____________________

Excerpt C mm. _____ ____________________

A Duet in One Voice

Find this passage in your score and play it. Then mark a bracket over each rising group of stepwise notes, and a bracket below each descending group.

What sort of pattern do you see? ______________________________
(CLUE: Think of a conversation.)

Where else does Bach use this pattern? ______________________________

In these passages, one voice seems to divide into two voices as in a duet. Listen to the effect of these round phrase-shapes shifting back and forth as you play them.

Form and Keys

The double bars and repeat signs divide this prelude into two sections.
Fill in the blanks in this form chart.

______	mm. ______–______	closing key: ______
		closing key: ______
______	mm. ______–______	closing key: ______
		closing key: ______

Bach's preludes usually travel through several keys and then return to the home key for the closing measures.

Name two ways to find modulations.

1. ______________________________
2. ______________________________

The second section of this prelude travels through a number of different keys.

Find five of these keys, label the modulations in your score, and write the measure numbers and cadence types below.

mm. ______	key: __________	cadence type: __________
mm. ______	key: __________	cadence type: __________
mm. ______	key: __________	cadence type: __________
mm. ______	key: __________	cadence type: __________
mm. ______	key: __________	cadence type: __________

When you have learned both of these little preludes, you may want to perform them together, either in a recital or simply for your own enjoyment. It is interesting to compare the two preludes. They have a lot in common, but there are some contrasts between the two.

When you have filled in this chart, you will have a useful summary of the similarities and contrasts between two of Bach's *Little Preludes*, and you will also begin to understand why Bach used them for teaching.

	Little Prelude in D Major, BWV 936	Little Prelude in E Minor, BWV 938
tempo		
form (binary, ternary)		
meter		
number of voices		
contrapuntal texture		
imitation of opening motive		
sequences		
note values (mostly long or mostly short)		
articulation		
character or mood		

Fantasia in D Minor, TWV 33:2

Georg Philipp Telemann (1681–1767)

Piano Repertoire 8 page 8

CD 8 / track 3

Telemann was born in Magdeburg, Germany. His lifetime coincided closely with two other renowned German composers of the Baroque period, Johann Sebastian Bach and George Frideric Handel. A composer, organist, music director, and educator, Telemann worked at various times in Leipzig, Frankfurt, and Hamburg. In 1723, he was offered the job of Kantor in Leipzig. When he declined, the town council chose J.S. Bach instead. Telemann and Bach were friends, and Telemann was godfather to Bach's son Carl Philipp Emanuel.

Telemann wrote over 4,000 compositions, including 40 operas, 44 passions, hundreds of cantatas and motets, and a large quantity of church, orchestral, and chamber music. He engraved most of his published works himself. His *Musique de Table* (Table Music), a collection of chamber pieces published in 1733, is probably his best-known work today. In 1732, Telemann published a set of 24 *Fantasias* in Hamburg. In typically prolific fashion, he added another dozen to the set in 1733! *Fantasia in D Minor* is the second work in the 1732 publication.

A Fantasia

The word *fantasia* (or fantasy) suggests a free style of composition. Many Renaissance composers wrote fantasias for lute, guitar, and other string instruments. From the Renaissance to the present day, fantasias vary widely, from free, **improvisatory** works to strictly **contrapuntal** works with sectional forms. Most of Telemann's fantasias have a clear form and an elegant musical style, but some also include chordal textures and sections that suggest an improvisation rather than a written-out composition.

Look through the score of Telemann's *Fantasia in D Minor.*

What markings divide the work into two large sections? ____________________

Which section has a more contrapuntal texture with patterns of repetition such as **imitation** and **sequence**? __________

Which section has a contrasting texture and a somewhat freer, more improvisatory and expressive melody? __________

The end of the *Adagio* section is marked *D.C. Presto al Fine.*

What Italian words is *D.C.* the abbreviation for? ____________________

What does this marking tell you to do? ____________________

Taking the *D.C.* into account, what is the overall form of this fantasia?

- ☐ binary
- ☐ ternary

First Section: *Presto*

Contrasting Texture, Integrated Form

The *Presto* section is written for two voices. Telemann uses these voices in two contrasting ways. You can see both in the first line of music.

What is the relationship between the voices in mm. 1–4? ______________

What is the relationship between the voices in mm. 5–8? ______________

When two or more parts have the same melody on the same notes, it is often called a unison, even though the parts may be an octave apart.

In a contrapuntal texture, each voice has its own melodic line, and there is a lively interplay between the voices. Sometimes each voice has its own motive, and sometimes the voices toss a motive back and forth.

Contrapuntal textures usually include imitation. The imitation may be either strict (that is, an exact copy of another voice) or free (an approximate copy where the rhythm may be similar but the notes slightly different).

Let's see how these two textures are combined by Telemann to create contrast and interest as the *Fantasia* unfolds (mm. 1–37). Use "U" for unison texture and "I" for imitative textures and indicate the key of each segment.

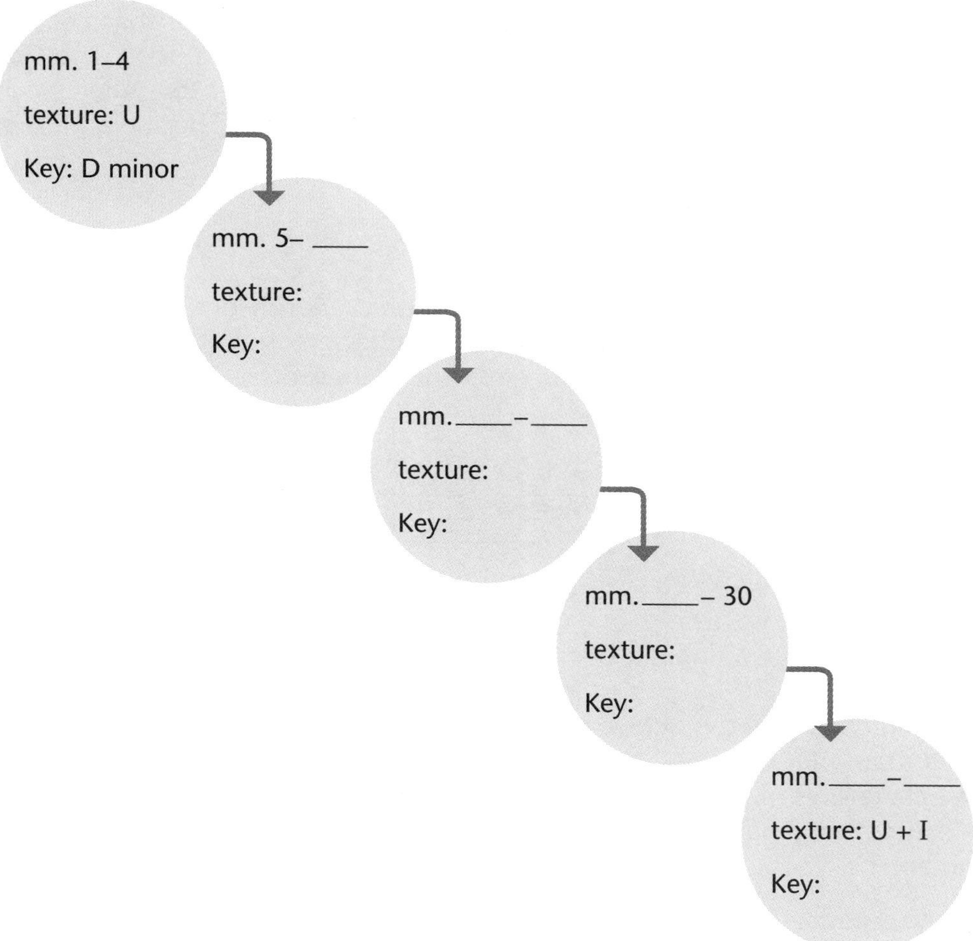

Contrapuntal textures often include sequences as well. Sequences create a steady forward propulsion and rhythmic vitality. They also emphasize the motive they repeat, so that the listener can recognize it more easily.

Where is the first sequence in the *Presto* section? ___________
(CLUE: This sequence also involves imitation between the voices.)

Where is there an upside-down version of this sequence? ___________

Composers often use sequences to **modulate** or to travel through several keys.

Find a sequence in which the two voices toss a motive back and forth as the music changes key. mm. _______________

As you have discovered, Telemann creates a lively and integrated structure by developing — combining and re-combining — his two styles of writing.

Like many of Telemann's fantasia movements, this *Presto* falls into two parts. Measures 1–37 alternate the unison and imitative themes, modulating to the dominant major key. Measures 38–78 develop the themes and touch on a series of related keys before returning to the home key.

What relationship can you find between the arpeggiated figure in the second part and the themes of the first part? _________________________________

Key Signature

According to the title, this fantasia is in D minor. You expect it to have a key signature of one flat, but it doesn't! In Telemann's time, composers often used incomplete key signatures for music in minor keys. Usually the last sharp or flat of the key signature is missing. This practice dates back to the use of **modes**. The **Dorian mode** (the white notes from D to D on the keyboard) is similar to a minor scale. Here Telemann has dropped off the B flat of the key signature, but he adds it in the music as an accidental.

Articulation

You can play the notes not marked with slurs *legato*, slightly detached, or *staccato*. Experiment with different touches, but once you decide on an articulation pattern, use it consistently each time the motive returns. Here is one suggestion for the opening theme (mm. 1–5).

The commas indicate a tiny but clear break. Hold the *tenuto* notes for their full value.

You may want to play the octave passages with a slightly heavier touch than the more contrapuntal passages. This structure is a little bit like a *concerto grosso.* Think of the octave–unison passages as played by the *tutti* (the whole orchestra), and the more contrapuntal passages as played by the *soli* (a small group of single instruments).

Did you notice that the *Presto* section begins and ends with the strong unison sound? _________________________________

Second Section: *Adagio*

The style of the *Adagio* presents a strong contrast to the *Presto*. Here, the expressive melody accompanied by full, rolled (arpeggiated) chords suggests a freer, more improvisatory style of composition. In Telemann's time, keyboard players learned to improvise accompaniments similar to this as part of their regular music study. The arpeggiation and decoration of these chords was an important cornerstone of this style.

Think of the RH as a vocal soloist, and allow the LH to provide an expressive, responsive accompaniment. These chords often come in groups of four. Linger slightly on the last chord of each group, and give the melody in these measures a thoughtful, introspective quality with just a hint of ***rubato***.

Harmony

The *Adagio* is in the **dominant** key of A minor. Telemann's harmony in this section begins with a pattern of tension and release as one chord **resolves** to the next, but he delays the **perfect cadence** in A minor until the end of the section.

Can you name the 7th chord in mm. 79–80? ____________________
(CLUE: In root position, it consists of three minor 3rds, and the interval between the root and the fifth is a **tritone**.)

How would you describe the sound of this chord? Does it emphasize the **tonic** of the key? ___________________________________

To what chord does this 7th chord resolve? ____________

Where is this pattern repeated? ____________

On his way to the final cadence, Telemann visits a number of different keys. Here is a list of the keys. Write the appropriate measure numbers after each one.

A minor: mm. ________–________

G minor: mm. ________–________

D minor: mm. ________–________

Circle of descending dominant 7ths: A–D–G–D–F: mm. ________–________

A minor perfect cadence: mm. ________–________
(CLUE: Look for the leading tones rising to the tonic.)

Invention No. 6 in E Major, BWV 777

Johann Sebastian Bach (1685–1750)

Bach's Inventions

Piano Repertoire 8 page 11

CD 8 / track 4

At the end of the *Notebook for Wilhelm Friedemann*, a collection of pieces J.S. Bach assembled for the musical education of his eldest son, there is a group of two- and three-part works called *Inventions* and *Sinfonias*. These were evidently intended as models for beginners in composition.

In an autograph copy of the *Inventions* from 1723, Bach describes these pieces as a teaching method for those who would like to learn to play two voices clearly. He stresses the importance of achieving a *cantabile* style of playing and an appreciation for how the inventions are constructed. He also states that the inventions illustrate how a good idea can be developed through **imitation**.

The term "invention" is generic — it does not apply to any specific musical form. Bach's inventions vary widely, but they are all based on the elaboration of a single idea. They all use imitative **counterpoint**, and they share a common **harmonic** vocabulary. In an invention — as in a fugue — the main themes are called subjects.

Counterpoint and Double Counterpoint

Music consisting of two or more independent melodic lines is called counterpoint. All of Bach's two-part inventions are contrapuntal — that is, each hand plays an independent voice. However, the *Invention No. 6 in E Major* has an important difference. In this invention, Bach uses invertible or double counterpoint.

Invertible counterpoint can be turned upside down — that is, you can move the lower voice above the higher voice (or vice versa) and still produce correct counterpoint. It sounds as if it is difficult to write, and it is! But for the composer, the performer, and the listener, it is also both mathematically and musically fascinating. Let's see how Bach uses this technique in this invention.

Two Subjects

Usually an invention opens with a voice stating the subject and a second voice imitating it several beats behind and an octave away. In this invention, Bach presents two subjects together in mm. 1–4. Play each one alone and listen to two different musical characters. (You might want to label one subject "a" and the other one "b" in your music.)

Can you name four similarities between the two subjects?

____

____

____

____

Do the two voices move in contrary or parallel motion?

____

Where does Bach first demonstrate that he has written invertible counterpoint?

____

Label the two subjects (a and b) on the music example.

Check mm. 1–4 and 5–8 note for note. Does Bach make any changes in either subject? ____________________________

Can you find two other places where Bach states the two subjects and then immediately flips them?

____

____

Balancing Two Equal Voices?

When you are learning a contrapuntal piece such as an invention, the first thing to do is to play each voice separately, section by section. This will give you an opportunity to listen to the character of each voice. At this point you can also begin thinking about how you will balance the two voices so that each melodic line can be heard clearly.

Contrapuntal music is usually described as having two *equal* voices. Is this really true? Think about the two subjects in this invention.

If you were going to label one subject as being more important than the other, which one would you choose? ____________

Alternatively, are the two subjects absolutely equal (in which case the question doesn't apply)? __________

This is an interesting issue to consider, especially in music involving invertible counterpoint. It is also important because it will affect the balance of sound you choose from measure to measure. The two subjects are quite similar. It is the differences between them that will help you decide on how to balance the sound. You can use this chart to make a summary of the contrasts between the two subjects.

Contrasting Elements	Treble subject (mm. 1–4)	Bass subject (mm. 1–4)
direction on melody		
length		
note values		
complexity of rhythm		
complexity of melody		
character of melody		

No matter which voice you prefer to bring out, each part should be absolutely independent from the other. Practice hands separately, and work on strengthening your fingers so that your coordination will be secure when you play hands together. Whatever you decide about these two subjects, make sure your listeners hear the results of your decision!

Form and Keys

The double bar and repeat signs divide this invention into two sections. Look through the music of the second section — or better still, play it.

Does this section have two parts? If so, where is the division?

____

(CLUE: Look for a repetition of the opening measures.)

Does this invention have a **binary**, **rounded binary**, or **ternary form**?

____

Make a form chart with measure numbers, and label the sections in your score.

Typically the music of an invention **modulates** to several closely related keys. If you know what these keys are, it will be easier to spot the modulations. Write the closely related keys of E major in the appropriate boxes in this chart.

Tonic key: ______	mm.	Relative minor of tonic key ______	mm.
Subdominant key: ______	mm.	Relative minor of Subdominant key ______	mm.
Dominant key: ______	mm.	Relative minor of Dominant key ______	mm.

Now look through your score, identify passages that are in each of these keys, and write the measure numbers on the chart. You may also want to mark the modulations in your score.

Another device often used in the counterpoint of Bach's inventions is the **sequence**.

Find three examples of sequences in this invention.

____

____

____

Articulation and Phrasing

When you play contrapuntal music, you can use touch to contrast the voices and clarify the texture. In Baroque music, eighth notes are often detached, while sixteenth notes and thirty-second notes are played *legato*. These are useful guidelines, but they are not written in stone! Always take the time to experiment with different patterns of **articulation**. Here are a few additional points.

1. Look for natural "breathing" points in each voice. They will not always occur in both voices at the same time.

2. Look for places where you can use a melodic, *cantabile* style of playing — it is not always appropriate.

3. Consider the tempo of the music. A touch that works with a slow tempo may not sound well when you increase the speed.

4. Look for changing roles in each voice. For example, in mm. 9–15, the texture shifts to a melody and accompaniment style. How will you enhance that

   difference in your interpretation? ____________________________

5. Most importantly, look for the phrases so you can shape each melodic line.

   How long are the phrases in mm. 1–8? ____________________________

   How long are the phrases in mm. 9–20? ____________________________

Sonata in C Minor

Third Movement

Giovanni Battista Pescetti (*ca* 1704–1766)

Piano Repertoire 8 page 14

CD 8 / track 5

Pescetti was born in Venice and studied with Antonio Lotti, an opera composer and organist at St. Mark's Cathedral. Following in the footsteps of his teacher, Pescetti wrote operas for various theaters in Venice between 1725 and 1732. In 1736, Pescetti went to London as a harpsichordist, and later he replaced Nicola Porpora as director of the Opera of the Nobility. The rivalry between this company and Handel's opera company led to the collapse of both organizations in 1737. Nevertheless, Pescetti continued his career as an operatic composer in London for another ten years, before returning to Italy.

Pescetti was one of a group of early 18th-century Italian composers who wrote keyboard music in a light, non-contrapuntal style which was very different from the music of their Germany contemporaries. In addition to his many operas, Pescetti wrote two collections of harpsichord sonatas. The first was published in London in 1737. The second, dating from around 1756, remained in manuscript.

A Brilliant Finale

This *Presto* is typical of most final movements of Italian Baroque keyboard sonatas. The almost perpetual motion of the continuous triplets gives it an irresistible rhythmic energy! The RH consists of a simple running figure, and the bouncy LH accompaniment is mostly single quarter notes.

Triplets and Phrases

In a first-class performance, each triplet figure will be even, secure, and crystal clear, and the lines will be gracefully shaped with dynamic color.

Notice the three circled skeletal notes.

These form the backbone of the phrase's direction. Here the phrase is directed upwards. These important notes repeat an octave lower in the second four-measure phrase. Continue to look for similar skeletal notes as you work through the piece, discovering its phrase structure.

Play mm. 1–8, and be attentive to the shape of each figure. Some eighth-note groups have a down–up leap, and others (marked with brackets in the example) move in a stepwise direction.

Can you think of two ways of practicing these figures to ensure that the stepwise notes are as clear as the leaps?

1. ______________________________

2. ______________________________

(CLUE: Think about different accents and different rhythms.)

Keep your fingers firm, and lift them independently when you are playing slowly. Be particularly attentive to the clarity of your fourth and fifth fingers.

Once the triplets are flowing easily, add a slight rhythmic inflection on the downbeat to prevent them from "running away." Play the RH alone and tap one beat per measure with your LH to provide a steady rhythmic pulse. Keep the rhythmic inflection light — strong accents will disturb the flowing triplet line.

Left-Hand Articulation

You might choose to use a bouncing, non-*legato* touch in the LH. As a general rule, play the LH quarter notes detached, even when they follow a half note.

In mm. 68–71, bounce off the LH eighth notes, but keep the RH fingers close to the keys. This will help you to keep the LH out of the way!

Dotted Rhythms

Which measures contain dotted rhythms? __________

In Pescetti's time, a dotted rhythm in music composed mainly of triplet figures would have been played in a triplet rhythm.

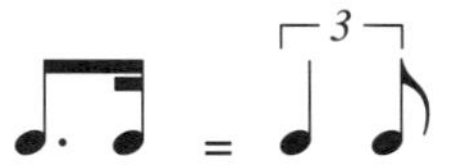

In this way, the "dotted" rhythm would fit smoothly into the triplets. You can see examples of this in the keyboard works of J.S. Bach. The triplet notation we are familiar with (with the italic "3") was not generally used in this period.

Repetition and Sequences

Pescetti uses repetition and **sequences** to spin out the triplet melody phrase after phrase. There are two main motives.

Where does Pescetti present motive "*a*"? __________

Where is this motive repeated in octave transposition? __________

What markings does Pescetti use to contrast the two statements?

____

Find the other statements of this motive, and mark them in your score. Look for places where you can use dynamics to provide contrast between repeated patterns.

Where does Pescetti present motive "*b*"? __________

This motive is immediately spun out into a sequence. How many times is it repeated? __________

Find the other statements of this motive and mark them in your score.

Is motive *b* always presented in a sequence pattern? __________

A Modulating Sequence

Play mm. 40–47 in block chords, then write a harmonic reduction of these measures on the staff.

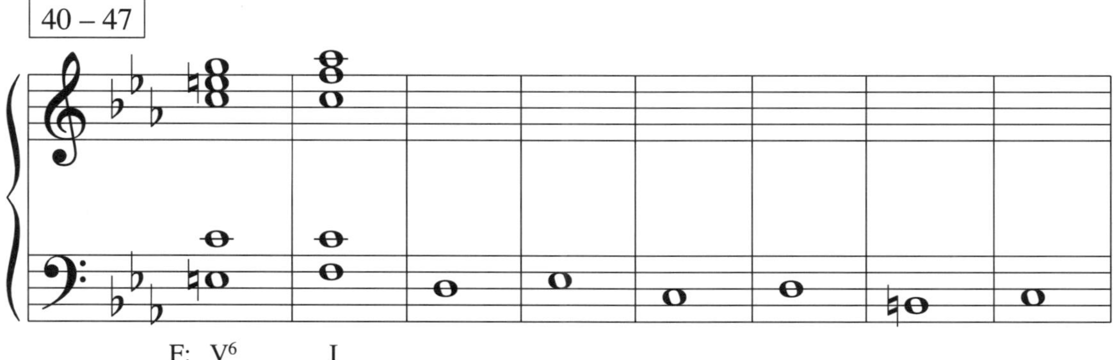

These sequence figures contain a chain of **cadences**.

What type of cadence are they? ____________

Identify the key of each cadence and label the chords. (The first one has been done as an example.)

This type of modulating sequence is a common Baroque device. What two musical functions does it serve here?

1. ____
(CLUE: Do you know the definition of the German word *Fortspinnung*?)

2. ____
(CLUE: Think of returning home!)

Form and Keys

For the full picture of the form of *Presto*, add measure numbers to the following form chart.

A	*a*	mm. ______–______	cadence: ____________	key: _______
	b	mm. ______–______	cadence: ____________	key: _______
B		mm. ______–______	cadence: ____________	key: _______
A_1	*a*	mm. ______–______	cadence: ____________	key: _______
	b	mm. ______–______	cadence: ____________	key: _______
coda		mm. 54 –______	cadence: ____________	key: _______

This shows the form is: **binary** / **ternary** / **rounded binary**. (circle one)
Each section or subsection ends with a cadence.

Find each cadence in your score, and identify the chords with harmonic symbols (I, V, etc.). Then add the type of cadence and the key to the form chart.

Sonata in G Major, Hob. XVI:27

Third Movement: Finale

Franz Joseph Haydn (1732–1809)

Piano Repertoire 8
page 16

CD 8 / track 6

For nearly thirty years, Haydn worked at the country estate of the Esterházy family of Hungary. During this time, he composed a wide variety of music and prepared musicians for weekly performances. In his early sixties, Haydn embarked on two highly successful and profitable trips to London (1791–1792 and 1794–1795). After his return, he lived in Vienna, where he led a quiet life until his death in 1809.

Haydn said himself that his isolation from the music centers of Europe forced him to become original. Thus, in many of his works we find fresh and innovative approaches, especially to form, with which he seemed to be constantly experimenting. His early keyboard sonatas (probably written for harpsichord or clavichord) were influenced by C.P.E. Bach. The *Sonata in G Major*, Hob. XVI:27 dates from 1774–1776, during the Esterházy years. This brilliant finale is a **theme and variations** and it shows Haydn at his best — full of vitality and charm.

The Theme: mm. 1–24

In a theme and variations structure, each variation has a different character. In the course of four variations on his theme, Haydn changes the rhythm, **articulation**, form, key, and accompaniment. However, the harmonic skeleton, the $\frac{2}{4}$ time signature, and the eight-measure and sixteen-measure length of the two sections remain constant. The movement is unified by the continued presence of the theme. For this reason it is important to present a clear, strong statement of the theme at the opening of the movement.

This theme has a joyful character. The fast tempo and rising melody create a spirited, rhythmic momentum that sets the style for the movement. The melody is made up of broken triads and 7th chords. It curves upward in mm. 1–4, and downward in mm. 5–8.

Where is the **sequence** in mm. 1–8? ____________

Does Haydn use this sequence to change key? If so, what is the new key?

____

How does Haydn change the melody in mm. 9–12?

____

Does he use the same pattern of 7th chords and triads here? ____________________

Where does the music return to the home key? ____________

The double bars and repeat signs divide the theme into two sections. Fill in the measure numbers in the form chart.

A	mm. ________–________
B + A_1	mm. ________–________

What is the form of this theme? ______________________

How does the A_1 section differ from the A section, and why do you think Haydn made this change? ______________________________

____

Variation 1: mm. ____–____

How might you compare the joy and energy of this variation with that of the theme? ______________________________

How has Haydn changed the melody? ______________________________

____

Are the notes of the theme melody present in this variation? ________

Circle these notes in your score, and give them a slight emphasis when you play this variation, so that your listeners will hear them clearly.

Variation 2: mm. ____–____

How does this variation present a contrast with the theme and with variation 1? Is it more brilliant or quieter?

____

What musical elements does Haydn use to create this contrast?

____

Are the melody notes of the theme present in the RH part? If not, how do you recognize this variation as being related to the theme?

____

In fast passages, it is important not to lose the melody in the sixteenth notes.

Write the important melody notes over the accompaniment for mm. 53–56.

What do these notes create when combined with the bass line?

____

Variation 3: mm. ____–____

Name two ways in which this variation differs from the theme.

1. ______________________________
2. ______________________________

Name two ways in which this variation resembles the theme.

1. ______________________________
2. ______________________________

What is the key at m. 81, and how long does the music stay in this key?

____

How would you describe the effect of this change of key and the subsequent brief **modulations**? ______________________________

How can you enhance the intensity created by tension and resolution in the **cadences**? ______________________________

This variation has a contrasting, darker tone. Bring out the sighing effect of the slurs. The 3rds of the theme melody are expanded to 5ths (mm. 83, 85–86), 6ths (mm. 89–90) and a 10th (m. 91). Give these larger interval leaps an expressive sound.

Variation 4: mm. 105–____

How does Haydn change the accompaniment in this variation, and what is this accompaniment pattern called?

____

____

Work on technical control of the LH so that the tempo and rhythm remain steady.

How does Haydn change the melody?

____

____

The playful character of this variation is evident in mm. 112–116.

How does Haydn use scales and chords to create a playful melody?

____

Can you spot a **dominant 7th** in this passage? Where is it, and to what chord does it **resolve**? ______________________________

In mm. 120–124, there is a sequence. What is the broken chord in the RH?

____

Are the cadences in mm. 114 and 128 the same? __________

Identify the cadences Haydn uses here, and write the chord symbols.

m. 114 __________ __________

m. 128 __________ __________

Be a Critic!

Every composer throughout the ages has been subject to the opinion of critics. Today you can find out the opinion of music critics in newspapers, on radio and television, and at conferences. In Haydn's day, critics also attended concerts and wrote reviews of new compositions in newspapers.

If you were a critic, which of the four variations in this movement would you choose as being the most interesting and why?

____

____

Which is the most challenging to play? ______________________

____

Which is the most innovative? __________________________

____

Which one do you like the best? ________________________

____

Theme with Variations!

This experiment won't work with every theme-and-variations piece, but it will work here because each section is the same length. If you have access to two pianos, invite a friend to join you. Have your friend play the theme over and over, while you play each variation. Do they always go together? Can you always hear the theme?

Sonata in B flat Major

Classical Period (1750–1820)

Domenico Cimarosa (1749–1801)

Piano Repertoire 8 page 20

CD 8 / track 7

Cimarosa, the son of a bricklayer, was born in Naples. His musical talent and good voice won him a scholarship at the Conservatory of Santa Maria di Loreto. His first opera was produced in Naples in 1772, and by the mid-1780s, he was Europe's most popular opera composer. He lived mainly in Italy, but spent four years at the court of Catherine the Great in St. Petersburg. On his return, he worked briefly in Vienna, where he wrote and produced his masterpiece, *The Secret Marriage*. This work was an immediate success, and is still occasionally performed today. In addition to almost 80 operas, Cimarosa wrote masses, oratorios, cantatas, songs, and keyboard sonatas.

Cimarosa's Keyboard Sonatas

Cimarosa's keyboard sonatas illustrate some of the musical styles which are associated with the period of transition between the Baroque and the Classical periods. The joyous, sparkling character of this music is typical of much of the music of the time.

Roccocco

Play the opening measures of Cimarosa's *Sonata in B flat Major*, then play the following three excerpts.

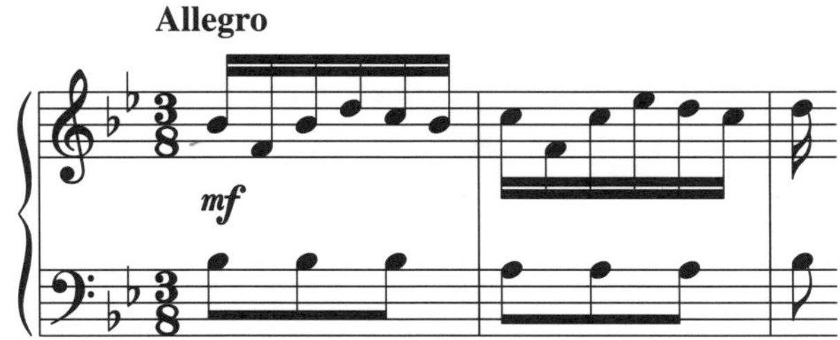

Can you name three things that these three excerpts have in common with the *Sonata in B flat Major*?

1. 16th notes in right hand
2. 8th notes in left hand
3. Key of B♭+

(CLUE: Think of tempo, melody, note values, character.)

You have just played excerpts from four different keyboard sonatas by Domenico Cimarosa. Almost all Cimarosa's keyboard sonatas are similar in style, and share a number of characteristics.

1. The tempos range from moderate to fast.
2. The melody is composed mainly of running sixteenth-note scales or broken chords, decorated with 3rds or multiple **grace notes**, and figures often involve movement back and forth in small intervals.
3. There is frequent use of repetition and **sequence**, and repeated patterns are enhanced with dynamic contrast.
4. The accompaniment figures are simple.

Take a look through the score of the *Sonata in B flat Major*. How does this description fit? Write your comments about each of the four points, and include measure numbers where these characteristics can be found.

1. The notes in the left hand change from eighth notes to sixteenth notes. The tempo is allegro.
2. There are many examples of this throughout the entire piece.
3. Similar patterns are repeated many times but in a different key.
4. Most of the left hand consists of 2-3 note chords.

The Basic Material

This one-movement sonata is built around the key of B flat major, with a few brief excursions to other keys.

Name the keys that are closely related to B flat major.

E♭+, G−, C−, F+

How many of these keys does Cimarosa visit?

all but E♭+

The **harmony** is also quite simple. The **tonic** and **dominant** chords appear in every **cadence**, and the main musical materials are scales and chords. The two principal themes are introduced in the first eight measures.

Mark in your book when you feel like you are in the key of G− C− F

Theme *a*

Theme *b*

Each of these themes recurs at least once.

Find all the statements of each theme, and mark them in your score. List the measure numbers and the keys here.

Theme *a*		theme *b*	
mm. 1-4	key B♭+	mm. 5-6	key B♭
mm. 23-25	key F+	mm. 31-32	key G−
mm. 25-26	key B♭+	mm.	key C+
mm.	key B♭+	mm. 07	key F

Where there are themes, there are repetitions, and where there are repetitions there are usually sequences. There is at least one sequence on each page of the sonata.

Find each sequence, and draw a bracket over it in your score.

Decorated Scales

Cimarosa uses the back-and-forth 3rds figure from the opening theme in several different ways.

Where does he use it in an **Alberti bass** pattern? most of the time.

Where does he expand it to 4ths or 5ths? ______________________

Where does he use it in a descending scale? Bars. 9 - 11

In mm. 11–15, the 3rds combine with the bass notes to form a **chord progression**. Play these measures with solid 3rds, and listen to the harmony. Then play only the upper notes with the LH line.

What is the interval between your hands? ______________________

The balance of these two voices is important. Experiment with different levels of sound for the upper and lower RH notes, and the bass. Notice the echo effect in these measures as well.

Hand Tricks

In the opening measures, your hands play quite close together. Keep your RH close to the keys, and allow your LH to bounce higher, so your hands won't bump into each other.

Find the two places where your hands are crossed.

Bar 11-12

Bar 39-40

Once again, keep your RH low and your LH higher in these passages, no matter what touch you choose for the LH eighth notes.

The motive in mm. 21–22 closes a section of the music.

Where else does this motive occur? ______________________________

In these measures, your LH chases your RH up the keyboard! Here again, the LH can bounce high to stay out of the way of the RH.

There is a piece by another composer in your *Piano Repertoire 8* that uses a similar motive. Can you find it?

____

(CLUES: This piece is in a minor key, and the motive falls instead of rises.)

Sonatina in G Major, op. 36, no. 5
First Movement

Muzio Clementi (1752–1832)

Piano Repertoire 8
page 24

CD 8 / track 8

Clementi was born in Rome, and by age thirteen he was earning his living as a church organist. In 1766, a travelling Englishman took him to England to complete his studies. Clementi established himself as a pianist and composer in London, and was soon recognized as one of Europe's outstanding keyboard artists. In 1798, he established a music publishing and piano-making firm.

Clementi's 70 keyboard sonatas and other piano music sold widely throughout Europe and had a decisive impact on later composers, including Beethoven. His collection of piano studies, *Gradus ad Parnassum* (1817), helped to define the piano idiom. Clementi's set of *Six Sonatinas*, op. 36, was first published in 1797. Clementi is credited with breaking new ground in piano technique as well as composition. His dazzling style, gorgeous *legato* tone, and enticing melodies captivated his audiences. The English pianos Clementi favored had light actions, and Clementi concentrated on independence of the fingers.

Perpetual Motion

A perpetual motion machine, once started, would run indefinitely because it would produce as much energy as it spent. This is a physical impossibility, but the idea was so attractive that it became a familiar theme of magic shows.

Many composers have used the idea of perpetual motion in their music; this sonatina movement by Clementi is a good example. Once the running triplet eighth notes are launched, there are very few resting places.

How many beats are there with no eighth-note movement? List the measure numbers here. ______________________

Is there ever a two-beat gap? ______________________

What sort of thematic character would you expect to be generated by such activity? ______________________

The Interaction of Tempo, Rhythm, and Meter

What is the Italian name for the time signature of this music?

____

How many beats are there to a measure, and what note gets the beat?

____

This time signature has a significant effect on the movement of the phrase line, and ultimately, the perpetual motion.

When you listen to the recording of this piece, do you feel the performer has captured the impetus of two-to-the-measure? ______________________

How will you capture that feeling of forward motion in your playing?

____

An Upbeat Grace

Since the RH upbeat "kicks off" the running triplet eighth notes, it must be played rhythmically and clearly. Before you begin, feel the pulse of the tempo you will play. Count a complete measure and then the partial measure, so that you come in with the upbeat in an absolutely precise triplet rhythm.

This upbeat triplet is especially challenging because it has a **grace note** attached! The trick is to prepare your fingers for it. Curve the third and fourth fingers of your RH before you begin, and "crush" the grace note firmly against the G, so that you land on both notes at almost the same time. You can practice this by playing a scale with an upper grace note on each note.

Sonata Form

This *Presto* is the opening movement of Clementi's *Sonata in G Major*, and like many first movements of sonatinas, it is in **sonata form**.

What are the three large sections in sonata form? ______________________

____

____

Harmony, **cadences**, and **modulation** will be your clues to the overall structure of this particular sonata movement.

Exposition: mm. 1–34

The exposition opens in G major, the home key.

Name the type of cadence in mm. 7–8. __________________

What accidental is used continually after m. 15? ___________

Find two patterns (chords, scales, or cadences) that contain this accidental.

mm. _______ type of pattern: ___________

mm. _______ type of pattern: ___________

What new key do these patterns suggest? ___________

Name the type of cadence and the key in mm. 32–34.

____________________ ____________________

How is this key related to the home key? ________________________________

Development: mm. 35–50

The development explores several new keys, creating a sense of heightened excitement.

Name the two triads in the LH of mm. 35–36.

____________________ ____________________

What is the key of the music at the opening of this section? __________________

How is this key related to the home key? ________________________________

Fill in the blanks on this map of the development section.

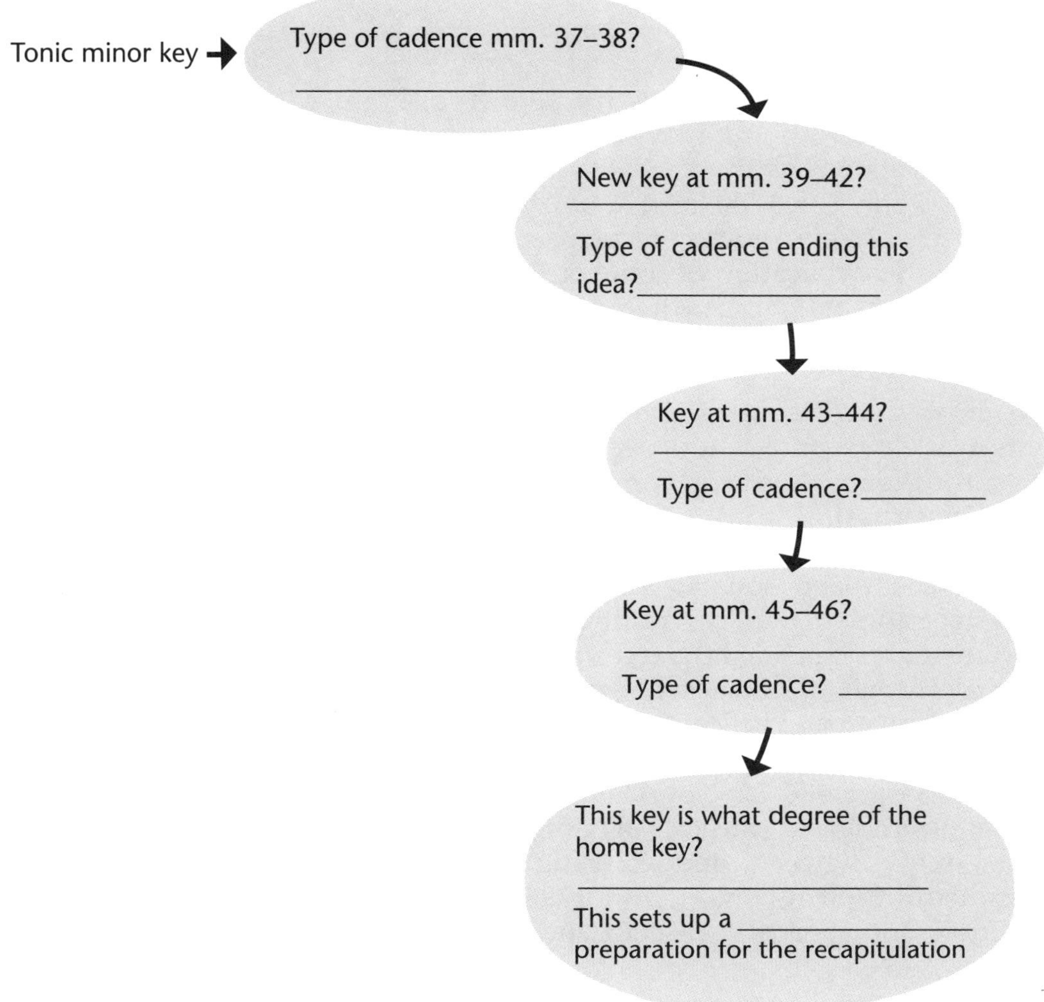

Recapitulation: mm. 51–84

The emphasis on the dominant prior to m. 51 sets up the return of the home key __________ , at m. 51. In the exposition, the music modulated from the home key of __________ to the key of __________. In the recapitulation, Clementi changes the music slightly so as to remain in the ______ key.

Keep Running!

Once you have learned this exciting sonatina movement, allow yourself to have fun with it. There is a piece by Giovanni Battista Pescetti in *Piano Repertoire 8* that also has running triplets. You may want to learn it if you haven't already. Both pieces are filled with vitality, and provide excellent examples of the innate energy of triplets at a fast tempo!

Sonata in G Major, op. 49, no. 2

Ludwig van Beethoven (1770–1827)

Piano Repertoire 8
page 28

CD 8 / tracks 9 & 10

Beethoven was born and grew up in the town of Bonn. Music provided a single outlet in his otherwise unhappy childhood. He practiced diligently, and at age twelve he was already earning a salary as a musician at the court of the Elector of Cologne in Bonn. In 1780 or 1781, Beethoven began lessons with Christian Gottlob Neefe. Neefe quickly recognized his pupil's talent, and in 1783 he arranged for the publication of some of Beethoven's early compositions. In 1792, Beethoven moved to Vienna, where he had composition lessons with Haydn and quickly established himself as a popular pianist and composer.

Beethoven was an innovator in his development of every musical genre, from orchestral works (symphonies, overtures, concertos) to chamber works (string quartets, trios, duos) and works for voice (Lieder, masses, opera) and solo piano (sonatas, sonatinas).

Beethoven's 32 piano sonatas are among the most significant pieces in the pianist's repertoire. Their composition spanned Beethoven's creative life, and through them, he expanded the technical, emotional, and dynamic possibilities of the piano. His piano sonatas range from dramatic to contemplative, spry to nostalgic, massive and virtuosic to concise.

Beethoven's *Sonata in G Major*, op. 49, no. 2 is relatively brief, but it is marked by several of Beethoven's musical signatures — vibrant rhythmic variety, active passages, simple lyricism, and dramatic flair — all held together through his clever structuring. It was written in 1795–1796, when the composer was in his mid-twenties and already well-established as a pianist and composer.

First Movement

Drama in Music

Many of Beethoven's later piano sonatas have a definite dramatic character. This shorter, earlier sonata has a miniature version of the same dramatic approach.

Beethoven was a master of orchestration, and the score of this movement suggests the sound colors of various instruments. Think of an orchestral sound as you learn the music, and write in the names of instruments that you think might play particular passages in your score.

Beethoven uses momentum to create drama.

How do you think the tempo and the triplet figures contribute to the dramatic character of this movement?

____

____

The element of surprise is dramatic. For example, in m. 15, the single melodic line accompanied by one chord per measure is interrupted by the pounding, rapid, contrary-motion triplets of the **bridge** passage — like an important character in a play making an entrance partway through the first scene. The bridge is in turn replaced by the serenity of the second theme in m. 20.

Register Changes

Register changes will usually catch the attention of a listener. In this movement, register changes have a dramatic effect — like an actor moving downstage. A change of register on the piano usually changes the character of the sound as well.

Where is the first register change in this movement? ___________

How does it affect the character of the sound? ______________________________

There are several more in mm. 36–52. Write the measure numbers here.

____

Dramatic Character

In drama, there are characters with contrasting personalities. In **sonata form**, the two main themes usually have contrasting characters.

The first theme is from mm. _______ to _______.

How would you describe the character of first theme? Is it outgoing, joyful, or confident? What words would you use?

____

The second theme is from mm. _______ to _______.

How would you describe the character of the second theme?

____

Does one character have a more colorful costume than the other?

____

Composers often use dynamics or articulation to color a musical character. Can you think of other ways to indicate the character of a theme?

____

Beethoven's Architecture

Beethoven is often referred to as the supreme architect in music. He planned his works meticulously and shaped them in his sketchbooks. It is also important for you, as a performer, to understand the structure of the works you play — especially in the case of Beethoven. This first movement is in sonata form. The following plan will help you to see the structure, and thus, to decide on your personal interpretation of this music.

Exposition: mm. ____–____

theme 1:	_______–_______	key: _______	character: ___________
bridge:	_______–_______	key: _______	character: ___________
theme 2:	_______–_______	key: _______	character: ___________
closing theme:	_______–_______	key: _______	character: ___________
codetta:	_______–_______	key: _______	character: ___________

Development: mm. ____–____

Name the last chord of the exposition. __________________

Name the first chord of the development. _______________

What is the opening key of the development section, and why is this key a contrast? ____

Which elements of the two main themes are present?

____

____

What other keys does the music pass through?

____

The preparation for the recapitulation begins with the **sequence** in mm. 63–65, where one key **resolves** into the next.

Name the chord in m. 63. ____________________

What is this chord in the key of E minor? ____________________

What is this chord is the home key of G major? ____________________

What chord is **implied** in m. 66? ____________________

Recapitulation: mm. ____–____

theme 1:	_______–_______	key: _______
closing theme:	_______–_______	key: _______
bridge:	_______–_______	key: _______
theme 2:	_______–_______	key: _______
closing theme:	_______–_______	key: _______
codetta:	_______–_______	key: _______

What is the surprising twist in measures 73 and 74?

____

What type of cadence ends the movement? ____________________

The *codetta* that ends the exposition and recapitulation contains a **pedal point**: the chords change, but the bass note remains the same.

What chord progression is used in mm. 49–52?

____

What chord progression is used in mm. 116–122?

____

Tonal contrast, rhythmic vitality, speed, surprising changes — all these contribute to the dramatic effect of Beethoven's music. Make the most of the drama in this movement. It is exciting — let your listeners share your excitement!

Second Movement

A Minuet and Trio

This movement has a Classical minuet and trio form, although the trio section is not marked as such. Part way through the Baroque period, around 1700, it became customary to join pairs of minuets together in an ABA structure. The middle dance was often labeled "trio" and had a contrasting texture and key. The minuet and trio was the only Baroque dance form that was carried forward into the early Classical era, where it developed into the standard third movement of the Classical symphony.

Beethoven wrote minuet and trio movements for a number of his earlier works. In the hands of composers such as Haydn, the minuet began to lose most of its definitive characteristics, and finally even its name, and composers such as Beethoven began to call their third movements *scherzos*.

This minuet and trio — from an early Beethoven sonata — presents a contrast to the dramatic opening *Allegro*. It has a lyrical, warm, graceful, dance-like character, and a varied texture.

Minuet: mm. ____–____

In the gentle opening measures, Beethoven seems to be preoccupied as much with melody as with the dance quality of a minuet. The melody shifts calmly back and forth between the **tonic** and the **leading tone**, before it opens out toward the end of the phrase. The dotted notes give a slight buoyancy to the rhythm, creating a lifting sensation on the upbeats.

How does the direction of this melody contrast with the opening of the first movement? ______________________________

Where does Beethoven use a shorter version of this dotted, stepwise figure?

____

In mm. 13–20, Beethoven repeats the opening melody. What term would you use to describe this repetition? ______________________________

The movement as a whole has a **ternary form**, ABA. The minuet section also has a ternary form.

Fill in the measures in this form chart, then play through the music. Listen particularly for the contrasts between the sections.

a	mm. 1–20
b	mm. _______–_______
a	mm. _______–_______

How would you describe the accompaniment in the *a* section?

____

____

What type of cadence ends the *a* section? ____________________

In the *b* section, which hand plays the melody? __________

How does the character of this melody contrast with the melody of the *a* section?

____

____

What is the function of the scales? ____________________

Play mm. 28–29. What key does the melody seem to be in at m. 28?

____

Name the last chord in m. 28 and the first chord in m. 29.

__________ __________

What type of cadence do these chords create? ______________

Describe the accompaniment figure in these measures.

____

Rhythmic Variety

The opening measures of the minuet are characterized by a dotted rhythm.

Where does Beethoven uses this rhythm to link two sections?

____

How does the melody resemble the opening measures?

____

Where does Beethoven use a rhythm that consists of quarter notes and quarter rests? ____________________

How would you describe the rhythm in mm. 28–34?

____

Trio: mm. ____–____

What is the key of the trio section, and how is it related to the home key of the minuet? ____________________

How does Beethoven prepare for this key change at the end of the minuet?

____

Parts of the melody are in double notes. What are the two intervals that Beethoven uses? ______________

____

How does the second voice enrich the melody? ____________________

What term would you use to describe the motion of these two voices?

____

What term would you use to describe the accompaniment pattern?

____

Legato cantabile

The trio melody has a vocal quality, and the slurs in the music are Beethoven's own. Observe these slurs, but at the same time, keep the music moving smoothly forward through the longer phrase lines. You can also enhance the melody by voicing the upper notes when the melody is in two parts.

Coda: mm. 107–120

Beethoven has written a short *coda* to round off the movement after the second statement of the minuet.

Why does this *coda* sound like a continuation of the main melody?

____

What other elements of the minuet does Beethoven recall in this *coda*?

____

Play the LH of mm. 108–111 in solid (blocked) chords along with the melody.

What is the key of the cadence in mm. 108–109? ________________________

What is the key of the cadence in mm. 110–111? ________________________

Playing a Complete Sonata

Although most of Beethoven's 32 piano sonatas have at least three movements, the two sonatas in his op. 49 have only two. In two-movement sonatas, composers usually create a strong contrast between the movements. In Beethoven's *Sonata in G Minor*, op. 49, no. 1, the slower and more lyrical first movement is followed by a spirited rondo. The *Sonata in G Major*, op. 49, no. 2 has a dramatic *Allegro* followed by an elegant, graceful minuet and trio movement.

When you have learned both movements of this sonata, you may want to perform the complete work either in a recital or simply for your own enjoyment. Together these two movements make a complete and satisfying musical composition that has not only variety and contrast but also a sense of unity. If you fill in this chart, you will have a useful summary of what you have learned about Beethoven's *Sonata in G Major*, op. 49, no. 2.

Sonata in G Major, op. 49, no. 2	movement 1	movement 2
Tempo Marking		
Key		
Meter		
Form		
Character or mood		

Sonata in A Major, op. 59, no. 1

First Movement

Friedrich Kuhlau (1786–1832)

Piano Repertoire 8
page 36

CD 8 / track 11

Kuhlau was born and raised in Germany. At age fourteen he moved to Hamburg to study music, and his earliest works were published there. In 1810, when Napoleon's troops invaded Hamburg, Kuhlau fled to Copenhagen. He lived in Denmark for the rest of his life. In 1813, he was appointed court chamber musician, and many of his stage works were produced at the Royal Theatre in Copenhagen. Kuhlau was also a renowned concert pianist. He was especially in demand in Sweden, where his pupils included many members of the Swedish noble families. The last years of his life were marked with tragedy. A fire in his house destroyed all his unpublished manuscripts and caused a chest ailment which led to his death.

Kuhlau's Sonata Form

Kuhlau was a prolific composer. He wrote orchestral, chamber, and vocal works, as well as theatrical music, but he is best remembered today for his finely crafted piano sonatas and sonatinas. This *Sonata in A Major* is from his op. 59 collection entitled *Sonates faciles et brillantes*, published in Hamburg in 1824. The first and the last movements of this sonata are in **sonata form**. The first movement has a typical late-Classical style. Its sparkling melodies and light, fast rhythmic figures call for clarity of tone, phrasing, and dynamics.

You can begin your exploration of Kuhlau's sonata form by identifying the three large sections:

Exposition: mm. ________–________

Development: mm. ________–________

Recapitulation: mm. ________–________

(CLUES: In Classical sonatas and sonatinas, the exposition was often repeated. This makes it easy to find — all you have to do is look for the double bar and repeat sign! To find the beginning of the recapitulation, look for the return of the opening theme in the home key.)

Follow the Opening Motive

Even a quick glance through the movement probably showed you how important Kuhlau's opening motive is to the structure of the work. Let's examine the motive and the themes more closely as they progress through the movement.

The opening statement is a charming example of musical dialogue, as short phrases answer each other. Measures 3–4 answer the first two measures, creating a sense of balance within the melody.

In the first phrase of Kuhlau's *Allegro*, how many pairs of answering fragments are there? ____________

Draw directional arrows showing each change of direction in these measures.

How do these changes reinforce the feeling of dialogue, or conversation, between the corresponding phrase fragments? ____________________________________

And now, follow the progress of the motive through the movement!

More answering phrases: Which *two* of the following effects can you find?

canon   echo effect   octave tranposition   melodic inversion

These effects, along with the silence which follows, create suspense as the ____________ends (which section of sonata form?)

Where is the cadence in these measures, what kind is it, and what is the key?

____

How is this key related to the home key of A major? ____________________

A surprising start to the ____________ section, in a key far removed from the home key ($\flat$VI). How did the previous excerpt prepare the ground for this? ____________

____

Development sections almost always include a number of **modulations**. Here Kuhlau passes through five keys.

Can you name them all?

1. ______________________
2. ______________________
3. ______________________
4. ______________________
5. ______________________

It's as though this sneaks up on you!

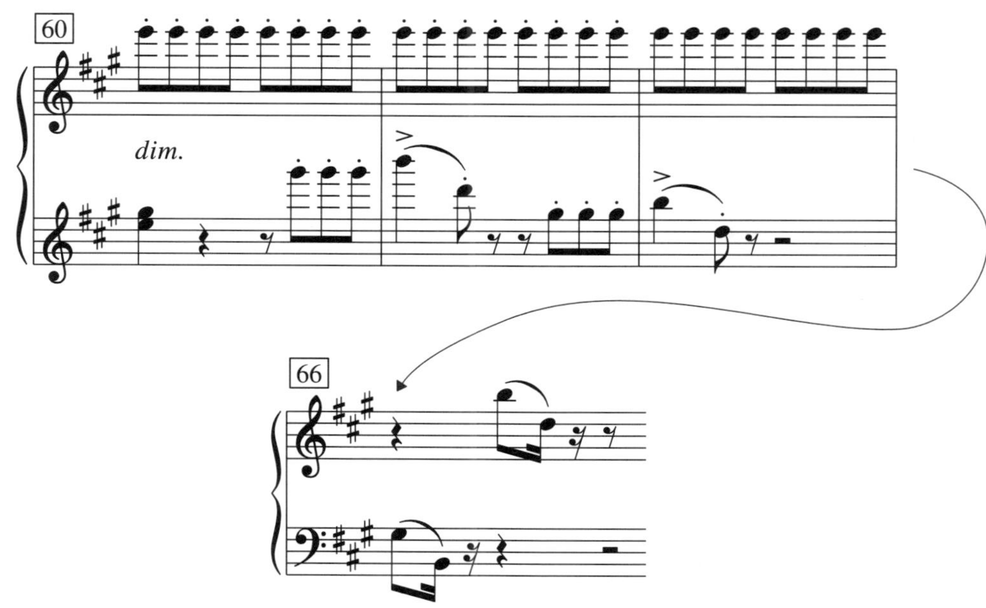

On which chord does this section finally come to rest? Discover it by arranging the chord in root position:

This is the __________ chord of __________ major. Which section of sonata form does this passage prepare? ____________________ As you play this, listen for the effect of expectation and suspense that it creates.

More Answering Phrases

You will find many places where short phrases answer each other in this movement, as you observed at the very beginning. As you play such passages, you will find many ways of making them convincing. At times, you may feel that some of the repeating phrases become more intense, others more relaxed, just as the tone sometimes changes in conversation between two people. Which of these fragments are followed by answering phrases?

Measures:	Answering measures:	
9–10	Yes	No
31–32	Yes	No
45	Yes	No
58	Yes	No
4 1/2 – 6	Yes	No

The Second Theme

Sonata form often highlights the contrast between the first and second themes.

What is the key of Kuhlau's second theme in the exposition (mm. 21–32)?

____

Does it present thematic contrast to the first theme? ___________

Does any part of this theme appear in the development section? ___________

In which measures? ___________

The second theme returns in the recapitulation in the ___________ key. How would you describe the mood of this return? ___________________________

Accompaniment Patterns

The melody is always in the RH. Let it sing out over the LH accompaniment.

Can you find two places where the RH plays the melody in the bass clef?

_____________ and _______________

Kuhlau has used several different accompaniment patterns.

Find three different ones in the music, write a measure each one on the staff below, name the pattern, and give the measure numbers where it can be found.

pattern __________________ mm. __________________

pattern __________________ mm. __________________

pattern __________________ mm. __________________

Prelude in B Minor, op. 28, no. 6

Frédéric Chopin (1810–1849)

Piano Repertoire 8 page 41

CD 8 / track 12

Chopin is one of the most beloved composers of piano music. He was born and educated in Warsaw, Poland. From an early age, it was clear that his only real interest in life was music, and his only real interest in music was the piano. He seemed cut out for a career as a piano virtuoso, but after he settled in Paris in 1831, he rarely appeared in public. Instead, he flourished in the atmosphere of the Parisian private salons. He made his living by publishing his music and giving lessons to wealthy pupils. From 1838 to 1846, he lived with Aurore Dudevant, a French novelist who wrote under the name of George Sand. After this relationship ended, Chopin's already poor health declined rapidly. He died of tuberculosis at age 39.

Chopin's Preludes

This prelude is from op. 28, a set of *24 Préludes* written between 1836 and 1839, inspired by the preludes in J. S. Bach's *Well-Tempered Clavier.* It is interesting to note that while Bach's preludes are arranged in ascending **chromatic** order (C major, C minor, C sharp major, etc.), Chopin's preludes are arranged in the order of the key in the **circle of 5ths** (C major, A minor, G major, E minor, D major, etc.) Most of the preludes are short and explore a single musical idea, but the styles, textures, and moods cover a wide range.

Character

The character of the *Prelude in B Minor* is one of dignity, with a slow pacing of the tempo and a long, expansive melody line for the LH.

If you were to orchestrate this prelude, what instrument would you choose to play the LH melody? a cello

What instrument would play the RH melodic figure in mm. 7–8? a flute

As your LH rotates slightly to the right for the top melody notes, think perhaps of a cellist drawing his bow across the strings. Try to imitate the warmth and resonance of the cello sound with a warm, round *cantabile* tone.

Melodies

Chopin uses two main melodic motives. The first, a rising and falling arpeggio figure which dominates the LH part, appears at the opening.

In m. 1, the broken chord lies comfortably under the hand. In m. 3, it is slightly extended — the second and third fingers cross over the thumb.

Name the broken chord at the beginning. B⁻

How many times is this motive stated? 4

Is it different each time? no

What does Chopin use to lengthen it in mm. 5–8? quarter notes

Where does the LH play just the opening fragment? bar 8

In which key? B⁻

The second motive first appears in the RH in mm. 7–8.

7

How does it differ in shape and direction from the first motive?

It goes down & up and and the intervals are smaller.

Where is it repeated and extended in the LH? bar 15-21

In mm. 7–8, the challenge is to balance the sound of the melody, the RH accompaniment, and the LH countermelody.

Harmony

The repeated B in the accompaniment figure in the RH functions as an **inverted pedal point**.

How do you react to this constantly recurring pitch as you hear the melody?

sounds like a bell - forboding? - warning?

What is the opening accompaniment chord? B⁻

How long does Chopin hold this chord before changing the harmony?

2 bars

When there are few chord changes in a passage, the effect is referred to as slow harmonic rhythm.

In some measures, the same chords are repeated over and over. In others, the harmony is constantly shifting as Chopin changes one or two notes from chord to chord.

Locate one such measure and comment on how you perceive the changes of harmonic color. bar 7, 15 The one or two notes make a big difference in the sound.

Can you find one or more places where Chopin uses **dissonance** to increase the emotional impact? bar 8, 6, 7, 15, 16, 18, 19, 20

Phrasing and *Rubato*

How would you describe the shape of the melodic motives? hills

What might you imagine to help you feel the expansiveness of each phrase?

____

Rubato — or rhythmic flexibility — is an essential part of Chopin's style, but it must be used with taste and discretion!

The rising broken chord seems to begin with purpose and direction, but it overshoots the tonic, creating musical tension before it relaxes back to it.

Where does the phrase want to move ahead? downward slope

Where does it want to linger? dotted quarter

Where does the melody transfer in the RH? Bar 6

Listen to the shape and expressivity of each phrase, and allow your ear to tell you when to make a tiny forward push or a *ritardando*.

Pedaling

Pedaling needs to be decided carefully in music where the LH plays a melody. In this prelude, think of pedaling by melody rather than by harmony. You will need to change the pedal frequently to avoid blurring, and you may want to experiment with half pedal. Here's an exercise to practice it.

> Place your foot on the surface of the pedal but don't push it down. Now play a repeated note at the tempo of this prelude. As you play, lower the pedal gradually until you reach the place where the pedal "catches" the sound. (This will be about halfway down.) Raise and lower your foot until you can find the place easily.

Now play the opening measures of the prelude, pressing the pedal only halfway down. Good pedaling is the result of experimentation, listening, and choice. This prelude provides a wonderful opportunity to practice good pedaling technique.

Comparing Preludes

Chopin's *Prelude in E Minor*, op. 28, no. 4, one of his most lyrical, also provides a wonderful opportunity for expressive playing. It has often been described as melancholy, and it was played at Chopin's own funeral. This prelude is included in *Piano Repertoire 7*. You may want to compare it with the *Prelude in B Minor*. The accompaniment patterns in the two preludes have some interesting similarities and differences.

Puck, op. 71, no. 3

Edvard Grieg (1843–1907)

Piano Repertoire 8
page 42

CD 8 / track 13

Grieg was born in Bergen, Norway. He studied piano and composition both in Copenhagen and at the Leipzig Conservatory. He returned to Norway in 1866, and settled in Christiana (now Oslo), where he earned a living teaching piano, performing, conducting, and composing. From the beginning, Grieg's compositions were well received and he became popular both in his native Norway and abroad. He had a retiring nature, and spent most of his later years at his home near Bergen, composing at a steady rate.

Although Grieg rarely used actual folk tunes, the influence of Norwegian folk music permeates most of his music. The rhythmic and melodic flavor typical of these folk melodies gives many of his compositions a distinctly Norwegian sound. Much of Grieg's orchestral music remains popular today, including his piano concerto, the orchestral suite *Fra Holbergs tid* (From Holbergs Time), and his incidental music for Henrik Isben's play, *Peer Gynt*.

Lyric Pieces

Grieg's ten books of *Lyric Pieces* were played often in their time, as they still are today. The 66 short **character pieces** found in these books cover a wide variety of scenes and moods. They also span most of Grieg's career as a composer. The first book, op. 12, was published in Copenhagen in 1867. *Puck* is from the tenth and final book, op. 71, published in Leipzig in 1901, only six years before Grieg's death.

Who Is Puck?

The name "Puck" comes from the Old English *pucca*, meaning "mischievous demon." Puck was a popular figure in medieval folklore and superstition, and he often appears in literature as well. By Shakespeare's time, Puck had evolved into a mischievous goblin, also known as Robin Goodfellow or Hobgoblin. There are a number of musical portraits of Puck. The character in Claude Debussy's *La danse de Puck* from his first book of *Préludes* is every bit as saucy as Grieg's!

The original Norwegian title of this piece is *Småtrold* (Little Troll). Grieg's portrait of Puck includes a lot of interesting detail. What do you think the following elements represent in this picture of a little troll or goblin?

LH *staccato* opening: ______________________

repetitive RH figures: ______________________

surprising register changes: ______________________

accents: ______________________

big leap (mm. 19–20): ______________________

harmonic tension: ______________________

Spotting Sequences

Grieg has based the first two melodic phrases on four triads.

Write these triads in solid (blocked) form and identify them.

	3 – 4	5 – 6	7 – 8	9 – 10
triad:	E♭ minor	________	________	________
position:	root	________	________	________

Now play mm. 1–10, and listen to the melody.

Do you hear a **sequence** in these measures? ____________

Now look for two more sequences: one in the first section, and one in the middle section (mm. 21–61).

Sequence 1: mm. ________–________

length of sequence figure ____________

direction of sequence (rising or falling) ____________

Sequence 2: mm. ________–________

length of sequence figure ____________

direction of sequence (rising or falling) ____________

Diminished 7ths

In the middle section of *Puck*, Grieg makes extensive use of **diminished 7th chords**.

Start looking at m. 21, and write down the first four you find. You'll have to look carefully, because some of these chords are missing one note. However, three of the four notes are enough to produce the distinctive diminished 7th sound. The best way to find them is with your ears! Add the missing notes when you write the chords.

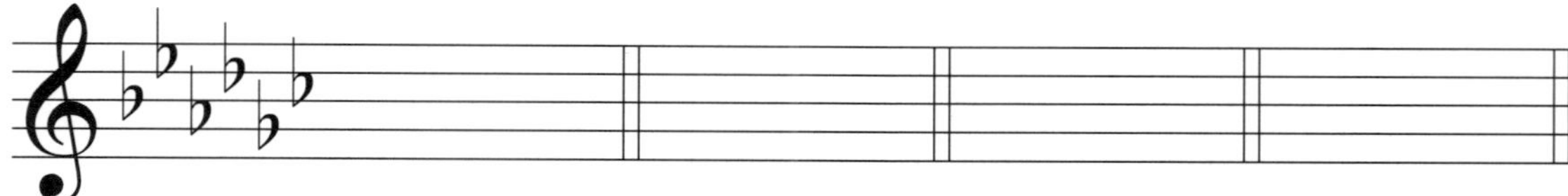

What atmosphere do these chords set in this section? ____________________

What do you think of as you listen to mm. 21–36? ____________________

What key do we arrive at by m. 37? ____________

What is your reaction to this tonality after having travelled through so many diminished 7ths? ____________________

Where does your imagination take you from mm. 41–60? ____________________

____

Composition Techniques

Here are three excerpts from *Puck*. Each one is an example of a composition technique.

Find each one in the music, and play the passage. Then write the measure number on the excerpt, and match it with the correct description.

Excerpt A
mm. _____–_____

Excerpt B
mm. _____–_____

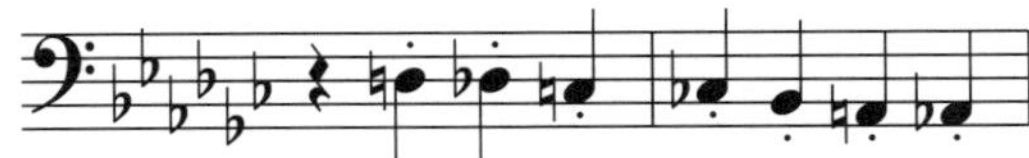

Excerpt C
mm. _____–_____

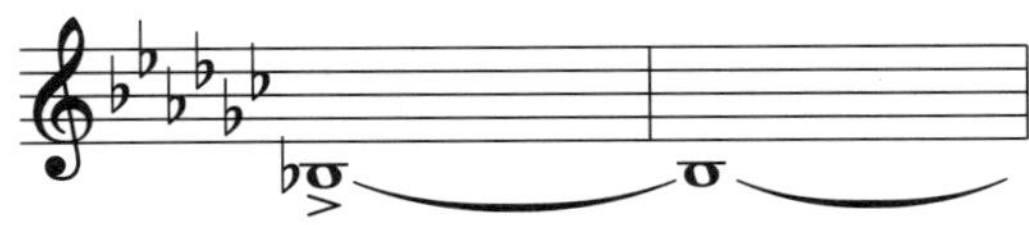

Excerpt ________ mm. ________–________: **chromatic movement**

Excerpt ________ mm. ________–________: **dominant preparation**

Excerpt ________ mm. ________–________: **cross (false) relation**

An Important Event, op. 15, no. 6

Robert Schumann (1810–1856)

Piano Repertoire 8 page 45

CD 8 / track 14

The young Robert Schumann had his first music lessons from a local organist. Schumann's father, a bookseller, publisher, and writer, encouraged his son to develop both musical and literary interests. After his father's death, Schumann studied law at the University of Leipzig, but he neglected and finally dropped his legal studies in favor of music. In Leipzig he studied piano with Friedrich Wieck. Later he married Wieck's daughter, Clara, much against her father's wishes. An injury to his right hand ended Schumann's chances of becoming a piano virtuoso. Instead, he turned to composition and music criticism.

From 1831 to 1844, Schumann was active as a music journalist. In 1833, he founded the *Neue Zeitschrift für Musik*, a journal which championed the cause of the new Romantic style. Schumann's critical writing, although not without its own faults and prejudices, throws light on his own creative process, and on the emotional and intellectual climate of musical Germany in the 1830s.

Kinderscenen, op. 15

An Important Event comes from a collection of thirteen **character pieces** called *Kinderscenen* (Scenes from Childhood) that Schumann composed in 1838. The music is written from the point of view of an adult looking back at various images and events of childhood. Each piece has a descriptive title that matches the music and evokes a particular scene or subject: *From Foreign Lands and People, Curious Story, Catch Me, Dreaming, By the Fireside,* and *Knight of the Hobby Horse* are typical examples. These pieces encourage us as musicians to use our imagination when we develop an interpretation of the music that will bring these pictures of childhood to life. This is an essential element in playing character pieces.

Think about an important event in your life. The music by its nature describes an event that is joyful, vivid, exciting, and powerful.

What other words would you use to describe how the music supports that event?

____

As you learn the notes, consider ways in which you can convey the real *importance* in the music through your performance.

A Brilliant Tone Color

The key of the music and the register of the chords give the opening a brilliant sound. Let's look at ways to extend that brilliance through the whole piece. First look at the texture of the writing.

How many octaves does the first chord span? __________

What **inversion** are the chords written in? __________

The use of the confident and warm 3rds along with the joyous sound of the 6ths creates a triumphant beginning.

What are the softest and loudest dynamic markings in the music? __________

What does this suggest to you? ______________________________

The tone of this piece is powerful, round, and resonant, but not harsh. Check that your elbow and wrist remain flexible while your hand supports each chord shape. Practice each chord in slow motion.

1. Feel the chord under your fingertips.
2. Drop your hand and wrist quickly.
3. Let your fingers descend right to the bottom of the keys.

The trick is to keep your wrist relaxed!

A clear ringing melody will also contribute brilliance. Here your fourth and fifth fingers will have to work the hardest!

How can you help these fingers to voice the top notes of the chords?

____

Rhythm and Accents

Although this music has a triple meter, it sounds almost like a march because the rhythm is so strong. The eighth-note upbeats should move the phrase over the bar line into strong downbeats.

Do all measures have the same upbeat? ___________

Those without the eighth notes may be played a little less strongly, to create one main pulse every two measures.

Schumann was deliberate about his accents as well as his bar lines.

Do the accents fall in a regular pattern? ___________

Are they always on the same note value? ___________

What effect does this accent pattern have on the meter and the rhythm of the music? ______________________________

The dotted rhythm lends character to the rhythm, and needs to be precisely and clearly **articulated**. Here's the trick: cut the dotted eighth slightly short, and hold the sound with the pedal. This leaves your hands free to play the sixteenth note with a strong yet relaxed sound. But remember — even though you are using pedal, your fingers must produce a clear dotted rhythm. The sixteenth anticipates the following eighth note. Try to play the sixteenth to the eighth in one gesture.

Playing Octaves

Does the LH play octaves all the way through? ___________________

How does this affect the character of the music and the sound of the **harmony**?

____

____

A detached touch will keep a bright attack on each note. The eighth notes can be made a little shorter than the quarter notes. Some of these octave leaps and scale passages can be tricky. Practice broken triads and scales with both hands —

especially keys with lots of black notes! This will help you to land accurately. The biggest challenge is in the **sequence** passage that begins in m. 9.

Work for accuracy by practicing the leaps alone. Notice the interval distance. If you really *see* that the distance is smaller in m. 10, that is the first step to accuracy. After many repetitions in your practice, try to play the LH passage in mm. 9–16 with your eyes closed.

In the middle section, mm. 9–16, accenting slightly at the first of each measure lends extra vitality and rhythmic momentum.

Cadences

This piece is probably a theory teacher's dream because of its clear **cadences**!

Can you name the four cadences in mm. 1–8? ______________________

____

____

____

Label these cadences in your score, and look through the rest of the music for more. There are two brief **modulations** in the middle section, ending with a cadence in mm. 15–16.

What is the sequence of keys? ______________________

What is the cadence? ______________________

Performing with Flair!

This is a great piece to play for an audience — even an audience of one! Think of ways you can make this music dramatic. Schumann's markings will give you some good hints.

Where are the two long *diminuendos* in the music?

______________ and ______________

How will you shape them — will you treat them both the same? If not, how will you make the second one different?

____

____

There are no special markings in the last measures. Do you think a slight *ritardando* would be acceptable, or would it stall the rhythmic momentum?

____

Consider all these things, and more. Above all, consider how you can make this music a really *Important Event.*

Andante sostenuto, op. 72, no. 2

Felix Mendelssohn (1809–1847)

Piano Repertoire 8
page 46

CD 8 / track 15

Mendelssohn was born into a prosperous, cultured family. He was a child prodigy, writing 13 symphonies by the age of 15. He later travelled extensively, performing and composing as he went. On his visits to England, huge crowds turned out to hear him play the organ at St. Paul's Cathedral or to see him conduct his latest choral work. He was the favorite composer of Queen Victoria. Mendelssohn educated his audiences in all types and forms of music. During his ten years as conductor of the Leipzig Orchestra, he performed works of Mozart, Beethoven, and Schubert, as well as music by Bach, Handel, and other earlier composers whose works had been forgotten. He was the founder and first director of the Leipzig Conservatory, one of the leading music schools in Europe. Tragically, his life was cut short by the tremendous demands he placed on himself.

Mendelssohn's music — symphonies, concertos, oratorios, music for piano and organ, songs, and chamber music — is characterized by clear expression and melodic invention. His *Songs without Words* present a rich, varied collection of short (but not simple) pieces which evoke a specific mood or scene.

Kinderstücke, op. 72

Mendelssohn's *Kinderstücke*, op. 72, a collection of six pieces for children, were published in 1847. In some editions, they are entitled *Six Christmas Pieces*. Mendelssohn may have intended them as Christmas gifts for young pianists he knew. No. 1 is dedicated to Lilli Benecke, and No. 3 is dedicated to Eduard Benecke. Unlike Mendelssohn's *Songs without Words*, none of the six pieces has a descriptive title. Instead, they are known by their tempo markings. The two pieces marked *andante* are similar to some of the *Songs without Words*.

A Singing Key

In music, each key has its own particular color and character.

What is the key of this piece? ______________________

Many people associate this key with particularly beautiful singing lines. For another example, look at the Chopin *Nocturne*, op. 9, no. 2, which is also on the Grade 8 list in The Royal Conservatory of Music *Piano Syllabus*.

Melody and Accompaniment

Does the melody begin from m. 1, or is this an accompaniment introduction?

____

What mood do you believe is set in mm. 1–4? ______________________

The melody of *Andante sostenuto* unfolds in a graciously flowing *cantabile* manner, like a song, carried by the RH over the murmuring LH accompaniment. Here are three steps to help you hear and establish the balance between melody and accompaniment. Start with the first phrase, mm. 4–8.

1. Play the RH melody alone and try to sing through each fingertip. Does each phrase sound like a voice or a *legato* instrument?

   ____

2. Play the LH lower notes alone, omitting the thumb notes. Can you hear a bass melodic line? ______________________________

3. Then, play the melody as written, along with only the lower LH notes. What is interval between your hands? ______________________________

4. Play the melody as written, and play the LH as blocked pairs of notes. (You will probably find it is easier to keep the LH notes quiet this way.) Bring the sound of the song to the foreground, and keep the lighter accompaniment in the background.

5. Play the phrase as written. Let the melody sing out with a warm tone, but at the same time, listen for the lower LH notes moving with it.

You can use these steps with many of the phrases in this piece.

When the melody divides into two parts (for example, in mm. 17–19), you will need to use voicing to bring out the top line. Your RH fingers must produce a different sound for each part.

Harmony

Andante sostenuto begins with a short introduction and ends with a brief epilogue.

What are the measure numbers of these two passages? mm. ______________

mm. ______________

Does Mendelssohn use the same material for both? ______________

Mendelssohn uses fairly basic **harmony**.

Name the two chords in the introduction, and label them in your score.

______________ and ______________

Brief **modulations** often occur in **sequences**. Find two sequences between mm. 14 and m. 18.

Name the **cadences** and keys for each figure.

1. cadence ____________ key ____________
2. cadence ____________ key ____________

There are other sequences and modulations in the rest of the piece. See if you can find them all.

Matching Phrases

Mendelssohn uses matching phrases to move the melody forward. One phrase is like a question, and the next is like an answer. Here are four excerpts from the music. Each one is an "answering" phrase. Find this phrase in your music, and play it along with the measures that precede it. Then add the measure numbers for the whole excerpt, and write the melody of the questioning phrase in the empty staves.

Excerpt A: mm. ____________

The question phrase introduces the **leading tone** of the key of ____________.

How is this key related to E flat major? ____________

This answering phrase introduces the **subdominant** of the key of ____________.

How is this key related to E flat major? ____________

Excerpt B: mm. ____________

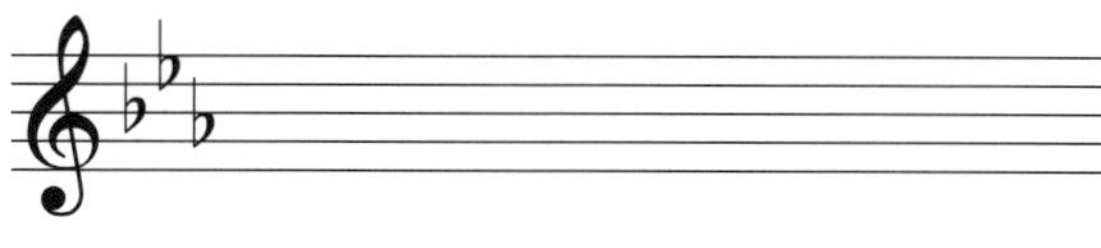

The musical flow relaxes here.

Is this a falling or a rising sequence? ____________

Excerpt C: mm. __________

The answering phrase is a slight variation of the questioning phrase.

Excerpt D: mm. __________

This phrase paves the way for the climax of the piece — a climbing melody over a **tonic** chord (mm. 33–34).

Is this a first or second inversion chord? __________

Do you know the chord symbol? ________________

How does this chord prepare for the final cadence (which Mendelssohn elaborates over several measures)? ____________________________________

____

Song, op. 2, no. 2

Bedřich Smetana (1824–1884)

Piano Repertoire 8 page 48

CD 8 / track 16

Smetana was Czechoslovakia's first great nationalist composer. He showed musical talent at an early age, and finally (much against his father's wishes) moved to Prague to study music. He earned a living, first as a music teacher for an aristocratic family, and later by opening his own piano school (with the help of Franz Liszt). From 1856 to 1861, he was the conductor of the Philharmonic Society in Göteborg, Sweden. In 1860, Austria granted political autonomy to Bohemia, giving rise to a new nationalist identity. The next year, Smetana returned to Prague, where he assumed a leading role in the new movement for a Czech national opera. Smetana wrote eight operas, the second of which, *The Bartered Bride* (1866), was the first Czech opera to gain international success.

Smetana suffered from a nervous disorder which affected his hearing. By 1874 he was completely deaf. In spite of this, he continued to compose. Three operas and his two best-known instrumental pieces — *Má Vlast* (My Country) and the autobiographical string quartet, *From My Life* — date from this period. However, his health continued to decline, and he died a few months after his sixtieth birthday.

Layered Textures

The generous phrasing and wide-ranging expression of *Song* is typical of Romantic piano music. To create a three-layered texture through most of this piece, it is important to coordinate your hands and pedal movements carefully. Notice how the texture becomes even more complex from m. 25, with four and occasionally five layers of sound!

Let's look first at the LH part. The LH obviously plays part of the accompaniment.

What other role does it have? ________________________________
(CLUE: Look at the LH notes. Are some more important than others?)

Play the LH quarter notes alone, shaping them into a *legato* bass line. Can you hear the bass line following the phrase lengths marked above?

____

Now play the LH part, mm. 1–4. Give the longer bass notes a little more tone than the triplets of the accompaniment, and hold them for their full value wherever possible. As you continue, bring out important countermelodies. For example, let the *tenuto* bass notes in mm. 15–16 sing out almost as loudly as the melody.

What are the two roles of the RH? 1. ________________________________

2. ________________________________

Now play the RH part, mm. 1–4. Play the melody notes with a *legato* touch, and direct more arm weight toward the fingers playing those notes. Use a light, almost non-*legato* touch for the broken chords of the accompaniment.

The accompaniment is shared by the hands, but it should sound as a unified whole — as one layer in a three-layer texture, blended into a harmonious whole with careful pedaling.

Finding the Cadences

Cadences are harmonic progressions that bring the musical line to a resting point — like punctuation in a sentence. When you have located the cadences in *Song*, you will have a better sense of the ebb and flow of the music. The following six excerpts all contain cadences. Write the letter of each excerpt beside the description that fits it best. After you have answered the questions, label the cadences in your score.

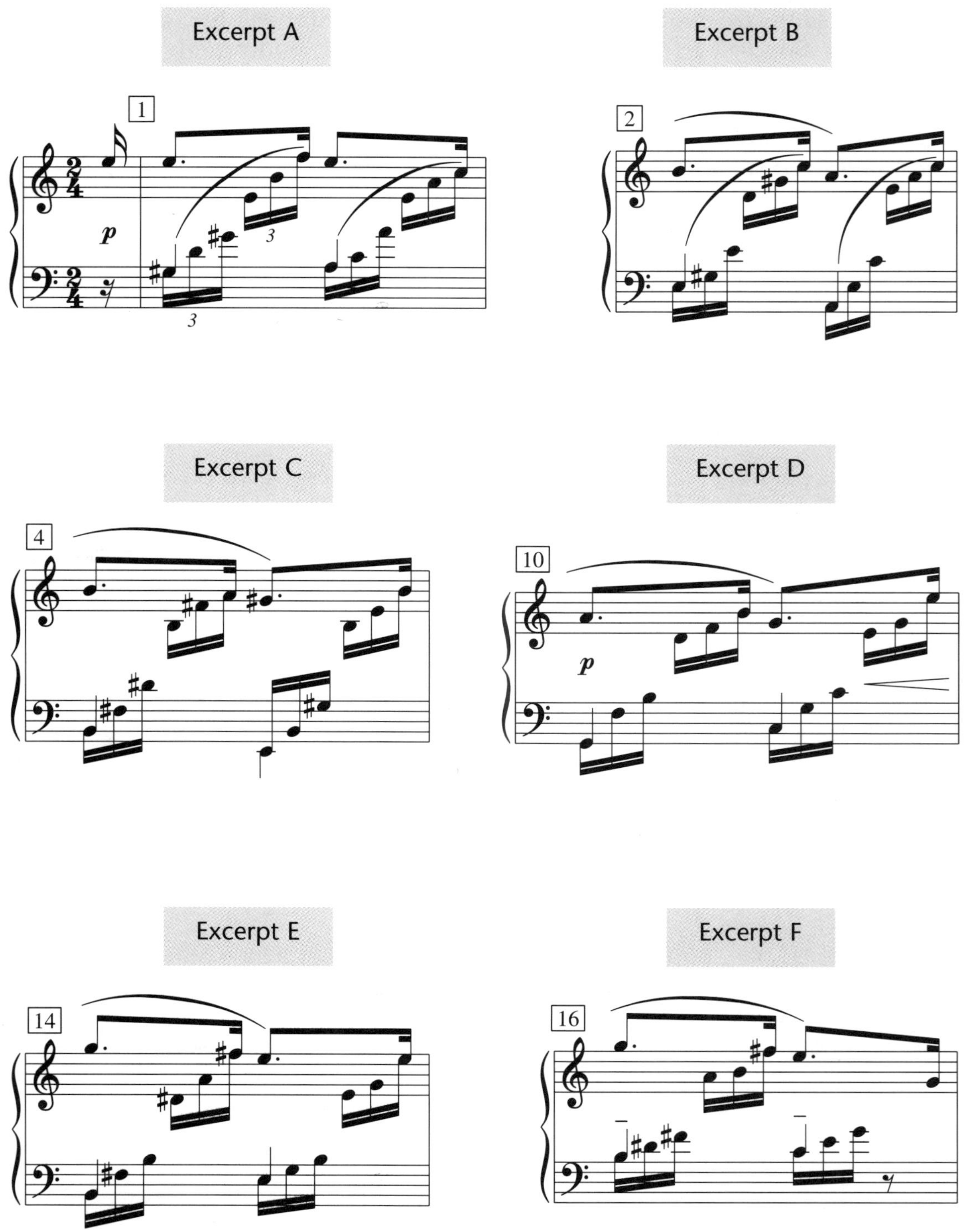

Excerpt _______

The second chord of this cadence is the **dominant** chord in the home key, but the **tonic** chord in the new key, _______ creating a V–I cadence in the new key. A minor returns in the next measure.

Excerpt _______

In this cadence, the bass moves from the dominant (V) to the _______________ (_____), creating a **deceptive cadence**. Play this measure. What is "deceptive" about the sound? ________________________________
(CLUE: Does the cadence end with the chord you think it will?)

Excerpt _______

This cadence moves from the dominant (V) to the tonic (I) in the key of _______.

This is a
- perfect cadence ☐
- plagal cadence ☐
- imperfect cadence ☐

Excerpt _______

In this cadence, the bass moves from the _____________(_____) to the _____________(_____) (fill in the scale degrees), establishing the key of _______ minor.

Excerpt _______

This **perfect cadence** is in the key of __________________, the relative major of the home key.

Excerpt _______

This **perfect cadence** is in the key of ___________ , the dominant minor of the home key.

A Few More Thoughts on Cadences

Now that you have identified a number of cadences, look at them in the context of the music.

Can you see a regular pattern? If so, what is it? ___________________________

____

This piece has a clear climax.

Where is the climax, and what five markings does Smetana use to enhance the effect of these measures? ____________ ____________

____________ ____________ ____________

Keep the relationships between the three layers of the musical texture in mind when you play these measures — this will help you to produce a beautiful tone.

Form

This piece has three sections.

Fill in the measure numbers and keys in the chart, and label the sections in your score.

A	mm. _______–_______	key: ___________
B	mm. _______–_______	
A_1	mm. _______–_______	key: ___________

How does the A_1 section differ from the A section?

____

____

What is the meaning of the Italian marking *con tristezza*? How will you change your performance to follow it? ______________________________

____

The theme of the A section follows a basic **harmonic progression**. Here is a harmonic skeleton of mm. 1–4.

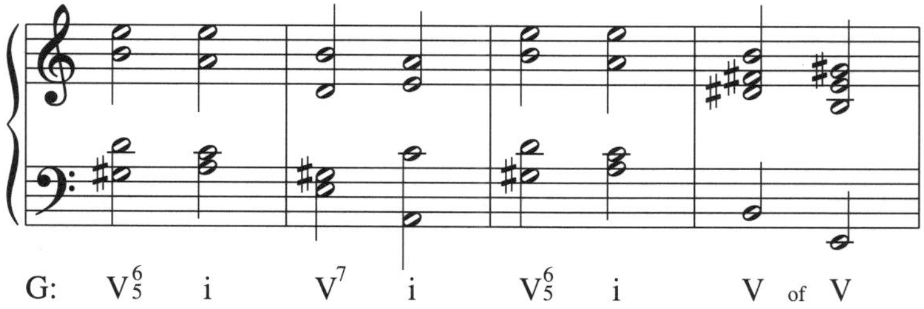

The B section moves through a number of different keys. Can you name the keys in these measures?

mm. 9 and 11: ____________

mm. 10 and 12: ____________

mm. 14–16: ____________

mm. 17–18: ____________

mm. 19–22: ____________

Consolation No. 1

Franz Liszt (1811–1886)

Piano Repertoire 8 page 50

CD 8 / track 17

Liszt was born in Raiding, Hungary. He studied piano from an early age, first with his father and then Carl Czerny, developing into a remarkable concert pianist by the age of twelve. In 1824, the Liszt family moved to Paris, and the young child prodigy began to tour Europe. Liszt spent many years as a travelling virtuoso, his incredible technique and showmanship amazing audiences everywhere. In 1848, at the height of his fame as a performer, Liszt withdrew from the concert stage. He settled in Weimar, where he became court conductor to the duke. It was here that Liszt wrote or revised most of the major works for which he is known today. Liszt was a great experimenter and innovator in his use of harmony and form. His music opened up new vistas in all areas, from increased technical demands to a heightened scope of tonal variety and color. His *Consolations* are among his most intimate piano compositions.

Experiments with Pedal and Sound

The *dolce* chords that open *Consolation No. 1* set the mood for the entire piece. The success of your interpretation will depend, at least partially, on your sensitivity to changes of harmony and the sound you can produce with these chords. As always, experiment to discover how to produce a specific sound. For these experiments, use a simple chord progression such as this set of E major triads.

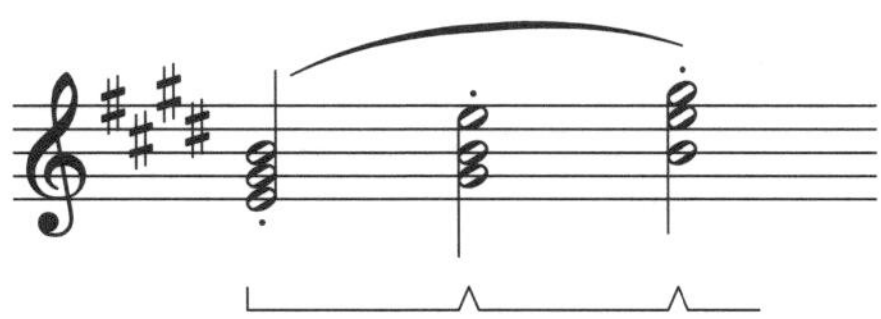

These chords have the same **articulation** marking as those in mm. 1–2.

The combination of a __________ and a __________ indicates a ***portato*** touch.

Portato is halfway between ___________ and ___________.

Now let's start experimenting.

1. Play the chord progression, and allow your fingers to float gently forward, off the keys after each chord. Listen to the quality of tone caught by the pedal. Is it gentle and warm as called for by the mood of this piece?
2. Repeat the progression. This time, give a little added ring to the top notes to create a melody. Again, listen to the tone sustained by the pedal. Does the top note ring out over the others?
3. Repeat the progression. This time, separate the melody notes from the rest of the chord, as shown in the example (and in mm. 5–6).

Keep the weight of the forearm gently resting on each of the top notes, and use a light *portato* touch for the lower notes.

4. Go back to the original progression, but this time, play quarter notes and use a ***tenuto*** touch. Let your arm weight rest on each chord, and move from chord to chord with a gentle but full sound. Try this at different dynamic levels, from *piano* to *forte*. You may want to use this touch in mm. 3–4.

Unexpected Keys

Much of the beauty of Liszt's music arises out of his free use of harmony and his juxtaposition of surprising chords and distant keys. In *Consolation No. 1*, he does all of this, and also uses **chromatic passing notes** and **suspensions** to enrich the lush harmonies still further. Play mm. 1–14, and listen particularly to the way Liszt uses harmony to give this music an intimate, introspective atmosphere.

Compare your reaction to the sound between mm. 5–8 and 9–16.

____

Can you find two examples of a chromatic passing tone? m. ________

m. ________

Can you find two examples of a suspension? m. ________ m. ________

Liszt further enriches his harmonic palette by using 7th chords.

Can you find two 7th chords in the opening measures? m. ________

m. ________

From E major at the outset, Liszt takes you to:

in the key of ________

The interval between the tonic of this key and that of the home key is a ________.

This type of **modulation** is quite common in Liszt's music.

Where does a similar fragment appear to "slip" down by a semitone? mm. ______

Write the triad of the key through which Liszt passes on his way back to the home key.

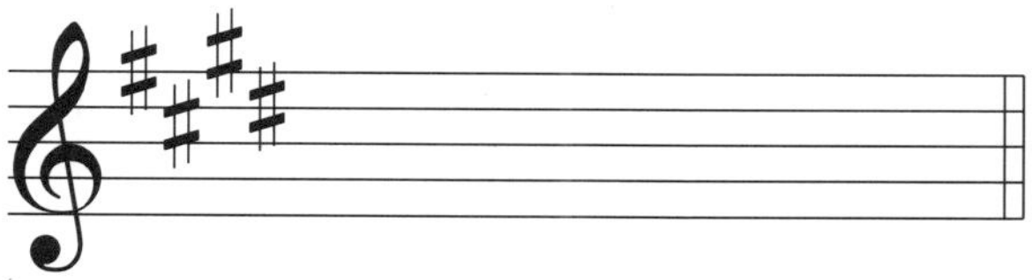

By what means does Liszt reinstate the home key? (Examine m. 17 closely!)

____

How does Liszt increase our anticipation for the tonic chord?

____

When we do finally hear the E major chord in m. ________ , it sounds all the sweeter!

Nocturne No. 5 in B flat Major, H 37

John Field (1782–1837)

Piano Repertoire 8 page 51

CD 8 / track 18

Field was born into a musical family in Dublin, and gave his first public concert at the age of nine. The next year, he and his family moved to London, where he studied with Muzio Clementi and was employed in Clementi's musical establishment. Field and Clementi travelled to Paris in 1802 and St. Petersburg in 1803. Field settled in Russia as a teacher and performer, living first in St. Petersburg and later in Moscow. In the course of a European tour in 1832–1833, he became ill in Naples, and by 1835 his health had broken down completely. He made his way back to Moscow, where he died two years later. Field's works include seven piano concertos, some chamber music, four piano sonatas, and a number of other works for solo piano.

John Field and the Nocturne

Field is an important figure in the history of piano music for his contribution to the genre of **character pieces**. His piano writing led the way for works such as Schubert's *Impromptus* and Mendelssohn's *Songs without Words*. When Field wrote his first nocturne in 1812, not only the name but also the style were strikingly new and original.

"Nocturne" is a title for instrumental works (usually for solo piano) composed in the 19th and 20th centuries. Nocturnes generally have a lyrical melody accompanied by broken chords. Field composed 20 nocturnes, but only 12 of them were originally entitled "nocturne." These pieces had a notable influence on Frédéric Chopin, who wrote 21 nocturnes for piano. The works of both composers share several characteristics:

1. a soaring, song-like melody line
2. a wide-ranging broken-chord accompaniment sustained by the pedal
3. a consistent rhythmic style throughout, in which melody and harmony are used in a fluid and often **chromatic** manner
4. the frequent use of **diminished 7th** chords

Melody

The long lines of the melody require great depth of *cantabile* tone and musical shaping. Play mm. 1–8 in four-measure phrases, and listen for the prominent notes of each phrase as follows.

Play the circled skeletal notes. In pencil, mark their direction. Note whether they remain at the same pitch, or move towards or away from gravity. Think of something that sinks with gravity. Think of something else that floats against gravity. How can you capture this in your sound?

____

____

Notice how each skeletal pattern is decorated by notes outside the pattern.

This melody is based on a __________ triad and decorated with upper and lower auxiliary notes.

As you play, you might breath in, toward each circled downbeat, and breath out after it. When you play these eight measures hands together, give the same breathing shape to the phrases.

Pedaling the Melody

As far as the piano is concerned, the 19th century was really the century of the pedal. Experimentation will help you discover many ways in which pedaling can help you to create the warm and varied colors of this music.

The $\frac{12}{8}$ time signature of the piece creates various groupings within the measure: two groups of six eighth notes, or four groups of three eighth notes (or, in the melody, four dotted quarter notes).

12
8

It is possible to pedal the first four measures by changing on each group of six in the LH. There is a general rule about pedaling that states that the pedal should be changed when the harmony changes (i.e., in the LH). However, in a piece with a definite melody line, it is often necessary to "pedal by the melody" rather than "pedal by the harmony."

Keep in mind that the harmony often changes very slowly in this style, so that your ear may suggest pedal changes within the same harmony in order to maintain the clarity and beauty of the melody. Observe the following:

m. 1: Number of harmonies __________ suggests __________ pedal changes.

m. 2: Number of harmonies __________ suggests two pedaling options:

1. ____________________
2. ____________________

m. 3: Number of harmonies __________ suggests __________ pedal changes.

m. 4: Number of harmonies __________ suggests two pedaling options:

1. ____________________
2. ____________________

Try the two options you suggested for mm. 2 and 4 at the piano. Which do you feel better helps you shape the phrases which begin/end (circle one) in these measures?

____

Harmony and Pedal Points

The characteristic LH broken-chord accompaniment of this nocturne is easy to play in its most basic solid (blocked) form. You can even use both hands to play all of the notes in the bass-clef chords.

What type of chord do you hear in the second half of the first measure? ________

Does Field use the same type of chord in m. 3? ________

There is one more chord of the same type hiding in the score! Where did you find it? ________

Mark the names of the chords that you know underneath the LH part. If you hear a **cadence**, write it in!

Measures 18–22 and 38–41 exhibit a texture often found in this style. The LH in mm. 18–22 is called a **tonic/dominant** (circle one) **pedal point**.

What is the reason it is called this? ____________________

The harmony (and melody) changes above it.

Observe the similarity of texture in mm. 38–41.

Which tone is repeated throughout in the accompaniment? ________

This is a ________ (name the scale degree) pedal. Does this, however, mean that the harmony never changes within this phrase? ________

Look for a chord which appears frequently in m. 38 and write it in root position:

Look for a chord which appears frequently in m. 39 and write it in root position:

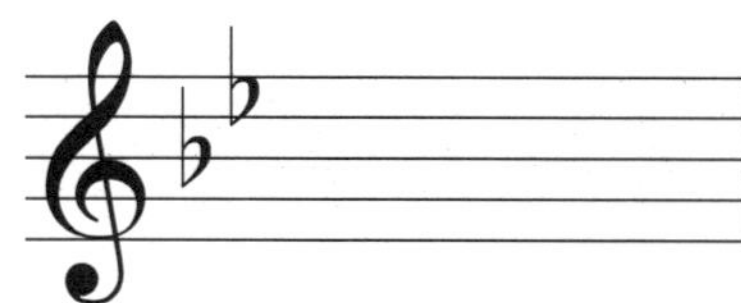

Does the pedal tone belong to:
- none of the chords ☐
- one of the chords ☐
- both chords ☐

How often must you therefore change the pedal? ________

If you find the sound becoming heavy or thick, experiment with some of the following:

1. Change pedal more frequently.
2. Depress the pedal only part way down.
3. When changing the pedal, do not necessarily clear away all of the previous sound if it belongs to the same harmony.

Decoration and Ornaments

Where does the eight-measure opening melody return in an **ornamented** form?

____

Field uses two types of melodic decoration when he repeats the main melody.

In m. 24, he writes a **syncopated** embellishment into the melody to fill in the rest that occurred in m. 2. (Here's the clue to playing this figure: remember that the LH F and D come first, followed by interspaced notes (R, L, R) until the next LH D.)

In m. 28, there is a small flourish — a group of notes played against the accompaniment notes. (Chopin used long, elaborate flourishes in his Nocturnes.) In this particular instance, the eight notes of the RH are to be played against six accompaniment notes. Think of this pattern as four-against-three.

These two melodic decorations are close together. The first suggests a delicate touch, but the second, following the *crescendo* in m. 27, suggests an increased musical intensity. Use a relatively light touch for both figures, to give them an **improvised** quality.

Chanson triste

A Sad Song

Piano Repertoire 8
page 54

CD 8 / track 19

Vasili Sergeievich Kalinnikov (1866–1901)

Kalinnikov was a Russian composer of the late Romantic era. He studied at the Moscow Conservatory and subsequently earned a living as a bassoonist, playing in regional orchestras in Russia. His compositions, including operas, cantatas, and symphonic works, show a personal and richly expressive lyrical gift.

Three Plus Two Equals Five

You have probably only rarely encountered the time signature $\frac{5}{4}$. Interestingly, it became popular among Russian composers toward the end of the 19th century and well into the 20th. For example, the second movement of Tchaikovsky's *Symphony No. 5* (the "Pathétique") is written as a waltz in $\frac{5}{4}$ time. Music in $\frac{5}{4}$ time has an interesting lilt that can best be described as "regular irregularity." How can you waltz when one of the two groups is short one quarter note? This is the wonderful, flexible character of this meter. The alternation of groups of two and three gives the music a lilting rhythm that is pulled just slightly off-center by the shorter group.

Explore the special musical feeling created by this meter by looking for details such as:

1. **Pairs of notes falling stepwise, in either hand.**

   Find three measures between m. 1 and m. 8 where these occur.

   __________ __________ __________

   In which *part* of the measure do these paired notes appear? __________

As you become familiar with this music, consider the effect of such details on the phrasing.

Do you feel that these falling gestures create moments of relaxation, or rather of increased intensity? ______________________________

2. **Rhythmic grouping in the LH.**

Play the LH part all the way through, listening particularly to the rhythm.

Do dotted half notes always fall on the same beat of the measure? If so, which beat? __________

Do groups of four eighth notes always fall on the same beats of the measure? If so, which beats? __________

Draw the basic rhythmic pattern as described above:

This LH rhythm is fairly simple — you will find only a few measures which are an exception to this pattern.

In this LH rhythm, can you hear a pattern of strong and weaker beats? _________

Where do you find the strong beat of the measure? ___________

Would you say that the second part of the measure contains an equally strong or weaker beat? ______________________________

In order to capture the expressive ebb and flow of Kalinnikov's *Chanson triste*, imagine tracing a large clockwise circle once per measure as you hear the melody.

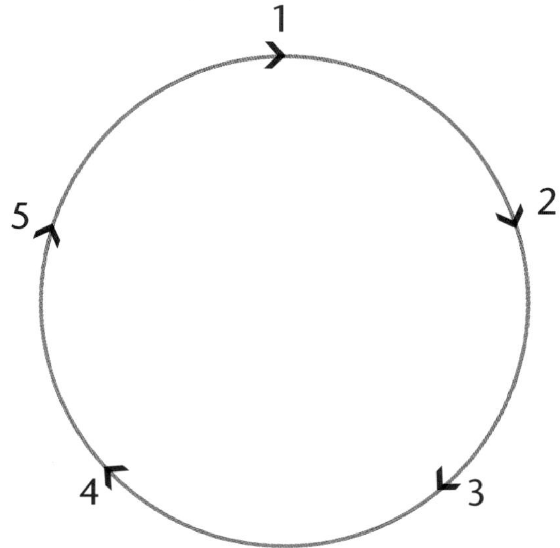

The circle should move effortlessly through the five beats. Notice how the motion never stops. Try to keep this constant flow of movement throughout each measure of the piece.

A Modal Melody

This music, as the title suggests, has a plaintive, emotive character.

Chanson triste is in the key of ___________. In this key, you expect to find the accidentals ___________ for the harmonic form of the scale, or ___________ for the melodic form. In mm. 1–8, the accidental ___________ appears in some measures but not in others. In those measures where the **leading tone** is not raised, the music has a **modal** sound.

Which form of the minor scale has no accidentals? ___________

Can you name a mode that has the same sound as this scale?

____

(CLUE: Check the list of modes in the Glossary at the back of this *Workbook*.)

This modal sound is characteristic of Russian music and arises from the traditional use of modes in Russian folk song.

You have already discovered the close connection between rhythmic pacing and melodic direction in this piece. Notice the **grace-note** figure, which generally falls on beats one or four.

What does this add to the rhythmical movement? ____________________

What does this add to the melodic curve? ____________________

In m. 7, the grace notes anticipate beat four by one beat.

How does this affect the design of the phrase? ____________________

Another example to consider is at the approach to the climax, mm. 15–16.

How do the grace notes affect the pacing of the phrase here? ____________________

____

Looking for Musical Sections

This Romantic character piece lays out its musical poetry within a simple form. You will easily find this form, which is very common in this style of music, through answering the following questions:

Is the opening section, which is in the key of _______ , repeated anywhere near the end of the piece? ________

Can you spot a section which establishes a different key center?

mm. _________ key of ________
(CLUE: The notes of its tonic triad appear here, shared between both hands. This is often a good way to search for a key.)

Consider where this section lies in the music, relative to the others, and choose one of the following letter-schemes to illustrate the form:

AB ☐ ABA ☐ AAB ☐

The name given to such a form is _______________.

Play the two opening measures of each of sections A and B, observing the expression markings. Although the rhythmic styles of both are fairly similar, do you feel a change of mood in going from one to the other? Describe the feelings each of these creates for you.

A: ____

B: ____

The B section is marked *poco più mosso*. What are at least two ways in which this marking creates contrast with the A sections?

1. ____
2. ____

Roda-roda!

Octavio Pinto (1890–1950)

Pinto was not only a pianist and composer, but also an architectural engineer. He was born in Brazil, and in 1922, he married one of that country's greatest pianists, Guiomar Novaes. Pinto wrote several sets of short pieces for young pianists. *Roda-roda!* is from *Scenas Infantis* (Scenes from Childhood), published in 1932.

Piano Repertoire 8
page 56

CD 8 / track 20

A Folk Song

The melody used as the basis for this piece is a South American folk song and children's circle game on the idea of "ring-around-the-rosie." The folk song is quite likely known in several South American countries. For comparison, look below at the opening of Alberto Ginastera's *Rondo on Argentine Children's Folk Tunes*, which uses the same tune. (This piece is on the Grade 10 list in The Royal Conservatory of Music *Piano Syllabus*.)

In both cases, the simplicity of the melody and the paired-note rhythm are characteristic of pieces based on South American folk songs.

Parts of the Game

The double bar lines divide the music — and presumably the game — into three sections. Label the first section "A" in your score.

Is the A material repeated in the third section? ____________

Are the two A sections exactly the same? ____________

If not, label the third section A_1 in your score.

Name three ways in which the B section provides contrast.

1. ____________________________________
2. ____________________________________
3. ____________________________________

Is this piece in **binary**, **rounded binary**, or **ternary form**?

____

Play mm. 13–14.

What do you imagine is happening at this point of the game song?

____

What clues does the **articulation** give you? ______________________

What does "*pp subito*" mean? ______________________

What effect might you try to create here and why? ______________________

____

What is the **interval** distance between your two hands? ______________________

The motion of these two melodic lines can be described as __________ motion.

Playing a Game Song

The phrases in this piece are quite short, with the kind of "question and response" style typical of circle games, dances, or rhymes. Since the melody has the rhythmical movement of energetic children singing, you might want to use a slightly detached touch in the A section.

Can you imagine the words being sung by a circle of happy children?

____

What articulation markings do you find in the A and A_1 sections?

____

How does the articulation of the B section contrast with that of the A sections?

____

Triads and 7ths

Pinto uses root-position triads in several of the pieces from *Scenis Infantis*. *Roda-Roda!* is based almost exclusively on root-position triads played with alternating left and right hands. Root-position chords also appear in *March Little Soldier*, and *Hobby-horse (Salta, Salta)*. These triads are very stabilizing and confident in their sound and they involve intervals of the 3rd and 5th, two of the most common intervals in children's songs. Pinto also uses these chords in stepwise patterns that give this bright-sounding music an almost two-part texture.

In mm. 1–2 and 3–4, the LH plays four consecutive triads and a 7th chord. Play these figures, and listen to the sound.

Why do you think Pinto included the 7th chord? ______________________

What term describes the movement of the voices in the triads? ______________________

Does the other consecutive triad figure (mm. 5–8) in the A section also move in a stepwise direction? ______________________

Compare the LH part of the A section and the A_1 section. Which triad figure does Pinto change, and what is the difference? ______________________

____

In the B section, is the texture similar to section A or different? ______________________

In which ways? ______________________

Does the texture remain the same or are there contrasts? ______________________

What do you think might be going on in this children's song from mm. 11–19?

____

Also in the B section, there is a more complex example of parallel motion. Play the slurred figure in mm. 11–12.

What type of chords will you hear if you play the notes on each beat as solid (blocked) chords? ______________________________

There are two similar figures in the B section. Where are they?

______________ and ______________

Does Pinto use the same type of chords? If not, what triad or chord do the notes form? ______________________________

Where does Pinto use solid (blocked) consecutive 7th chords? ______________

Do they create a **dissonant** sound? __________

The End of the Game

Although the A_1 section is much like the A section, Pinto adds a number of elements to intensify the final moments of the game song. Play the two sections through, and listen for differences in articulation and dynamics as well as in the notes themselves. Now take a closer look at the A_1 section.

Find the parallel octaves "filled in" with 5ths. What does this figure replace in the A section? ______________________________

Why do you think Pinto varied them in this way? ______________________

What other difference can you find between the two measures?

____

Where does Pinto use broken octaves, and what do they replace in the A section?

____

What do these octaves add to the energy of the music? __________________

Other than changing the notes, how does Pinto add excitement in the last three measures?____

____

What is the Italian word that implies a race to the end? __________________

Evening at the Village

Béla Bartók (1881–1945)

Piano Repertoire 8 page 58

CD 8 / track 21

Bartók was born in a small Hungarian village. His parents encouraged his love of music at an early age, and he gave his first concert at the age of 11. Later he became a famous pianist, teacher, and composer. As a young man, Bartók was swept up in the Hungarian nationalist movement of the time, and became keenly interested in Hungarian folk tunes. In 1906, he made his first field trip to collect folk songs, and soon after, began his scholarly writings on the subject. With the invention of the phonograph, he was able to record thousands of folk songs from singers in small villages in Hungary, Romania, Ukraine, Bulgaria, and Turkey. In 1940, Bartók moved to the United States, where he lived until his death.

Bartók's interest in folk music and teaching led him to compose several large collections of pieces through which students could explore different aspects of these folk tunes. *Evening at the Village* (variously published as *Evening in the Country* or *Evening in Transylvania*) is from *Ten Easy Pieces*, published in Hungary in 1909. Transylvania is now part of Romania, but when this piece was written, it was part of Hungary.

Two Contrasting Styles

This piece is built on two highly contrasting but typical styles of Hungarian folk music. Bartók makes their layout clear by marking two specific headings throughout the piece, which give you a general sense of what to expect.

Draw lines to match each feature listed in the right-hand column with the appropriate heading in the left-hand column.

		playful or dance-like character
		flexible pulse
1.	***Lento, rubato***	fast tempo
		emphasis on melody
		storytelling or song-like character
		sustained notes
		many short notes
2.	***Vivo, non rubato***	steady pulse
		slow tempo
		emphasis on rhythm

An Arch Form

The alternation between *Lento, rubato* and *Vivo, non rubato* sections creates an arch form.

Fill in the measure numbers for each section, and add a small "1" (or "2" if necessary) to indicate a section that is similar but not identical.

A	B	A	B	A
mm. ___–___	mm. ___–___	mm. ___–___	mm. ___–___	mm. ___–___

In Classical music, the sound usually relaxes at the ends of phrases.

What happens in this piece? What effect do Bartók's **articulation** markings have on the last notes of the phrases?

____

Telling the Story

The alternation of the two styles imitates a traditional manner of storytelling from the countryside that was half spoken in a free rhythm, and half sung. Play each section through, and think about a storyline that might be behind the music.

A

The first *lento* section one (mm. 1–9) is like an introduction — it sets the mood, and describes the place, time, and characters.

What mood does this section set for you? ____________________

Write a few words or phrases that outline your idea of the introduction to the tale.

____

____

Notice the frequent use of 3rds, an expressive interval frequently used in folk songs. Three of the phrases end on a 3rd marked with special markings.

Name each marking and describe how you might color that note.

1. __________ ________________________
2. __________ ________________________

What do you think Bartók is trying to achieve through these sounds?

____

The first two phrases begin similarly, with a marking over the first note.

What special musical quality is given to this note as the phrase opens?

____

Lastly, play the lowest LH notes in the first section.

What does this pattern form? ____________________

The pattern descends right to the end of the section. How does this affect the mood of the section? ______________________________

B

In the first *vivo* section, there seems to be a change of energy!

What is happening? ____________________

What do you see in the notation that suggests your idea? ____________________

At the end, what is the meaning of the whole measure rest?

____

A_1

The second *lento* section (mm. 21–29) is not quite the same as the first.

How has Bartók changed the **harmony**? How does this affect the sound?

____

How has he changed the rhythm? How has that affected the sense of movement?

____

What is happening in your story?

____

____

B_1

The second *vivo* section (mm. 30–41) is also different from the first.

What does the high register of the melody represent?

____

A_2

Does this section contain the most intense dynamic levels? ____________

When you tell a story with high intensity, how do you feel? ____________________

Imagine this feeling as you play this section.

In this section, how does the presentation of the melody differ from the first *lento* section?

____

How does the accompaniment differ?

____

What do these changes represent in your story?

____

____

A Traditional Instrument

In the last *lento* section, the melody is accompanied by repeated, gently ringing chords. This is an imitation of the sound of a *cimbalom* — a traditional Hungarian dulcimer. The plucking of the strings with a plectrum gives a sweet and slightly twangy sound.

A Traditional Scale

Play the melodies of both the *lento* and the *vivo* sections, and listen particularly to the notes that Bartók has chosen.

Do these two melodies have a similar sound? ___________

Build a scale from the notes of the melody of the *lento* section.

How many notes are there in the scale? ___________

What term would you use to describe this scale? ___________________

This scale can be found not only in folk music from central and southern Europe, but also in various cultures through the Middle East and Asia.

Is the melody of the *vivo* sections based on the same scale? ___________

A Syncopated Rhythm

Bartók uses **syncopated** rhythms in both sections. Look for rhythms in which notes are played between the beats and held through the next beat.

Write one syncopated rhythm from each section of the piece.

____

____

____

____

____

O Moon

Alexina Louie (1949–)

Piano Repertoire 8 page 60

CD 8 / track 22

Alexina Louie is a Canadian composer of international reputation. She has been commissioned to write major works for many of Canada's leading performers, ensembles, and orchestras, and her solo keyboard works are included on many competition and syllabus lists. Louie has developed a uniquely personal, expressive style, rooted in a blend of East and West musical traditions. Her music emphasizes both craft and imagination, and influences range from her Chinese heritage to an ongoing investigation of literature, poetry, and the visual arts. Louie currently resides in Toronto, where she continues her work as a composer, writing for all media including dance, film, and television. *O Moon* is from a collection of intermediate piano pieces entitled *Star Light, Star Bright.*

Contemporary Notation

You may find some of the notation in this piece a little unusual. Contemporary composers often have to create new ways of writing traditional music notation in order to express the specific sounds they want. These comments, written by Alexina Louie, have been excerpted from the introduction to *Star Light, Star Bright.*

> The nine pieces that make up *Star Light, Star Bright* are meant to introduce intermediate-level pianists to contemporary music . . . The works do make use of a range of contemporary techniques, including proportional notation (bar lines are eliminated), rapidly repeated figures which create a shimmering effect, chord clusters, and grace-note phrases (to be played as quickly as possible). . .
>
> Where meter changes occur, bear in mind that the eighth note remains constant. Tempo markings and durational markings in seconds for *senza misura* (without measure) sections are approximate. *Una corda* markings are suggested (one might omit them, or add more) . . .
>
> Accidentals hold through the measure in metered sections. In *senza misura* sections, accidentals apply only to the note they immediately precede and only in the octave in which they appear, except in the case of repeated notes, which are all governed by the accidental.

Exploring the Title

Contemporary artists often choose titles for paintings and sculptures that communicate an idea or an impression of the work — these titles draw the viewer closer to the work and to the ideas the artist is attempting to convey. Contemporary composers title their works with the same intention.

The title — *O Moon* — can lead you into the music, and also into the type of sound Louie has created to express her ideas. The title itself also has meaning. Say it out loud, and listen to the sound of your voice.

Could the "*O*" be a visual representation of the moon?

____

Is someone addressing the moon through this music?

____

Exploring the Sound

O Moon creates an evocative, atmospheric sound picture. For an exquisite introduction to this sound, play mm. 12–13, and use the pedal as indicated in the score. Allow the sound of the top notes to ring out of the piano like bells, and listen for the way their sound floats above the lower pitches.

Think about a connection between this sound and the title *O Moon*.

Describe the picture this sound brings to your mind.

____

____

____

Your performance can communicate your picture to your listeners. Think about how you can translate your interpretation into subtleties of touch and dynamics — into the language of music.

Keep experimenting with the sound, and look for different ways to vary the tonal color. Keep trying different degrees of pedaling as well, until you get exactly the effect you want.

Grace-Note Phrases

According to Louie's instructions, the grace-note phrases in the third line of the music are played rapidly, or as fast as possible! Since these figures are divided between the hands, it is fairly easy to play evenly and quickly.

What type of scale do these phrases form? ____________________

Cluster Chords

This piece is all about tonal color. Play the *8va* chords in the first line of music, and listen to the color of the sounds they produce. A group of notes played together with no particular tonality involved is called a **cluster chord** or a **tone cluster**.

Play the chords in this example, then find them in the music.

Now play the RH chords alone. Do you recognize any of these triads or 7th chords? Write the names above the chords you can identify.

Now play the LH alone, then write the names of the chords on the example. (CLUE: These chords will be easier to name if you go by the sound of the notes, or the look of the piano keys, rather than by their appearance in the score. Think about **enharmonic** changes.)

When you play these chords hands together, decide which notes you want to highlight in terms of sound. There are a number of different possibilities. As usual, experimentation is the best way to find out, and it will also help your chord technique!

Can you describe the sound you hear? ______________________________

Here's an example of cluster chords in **sequence**.

Find this excerpt in the music and play it.
(CLUE: Remember Louie's instruction about accidentals in *senza misura* sections.)

These clusters gather notes one note at a time — like rolling a ball of snow to make a snow-person! Circle the series of descending notes, then play them.

Where have you seen — and heard — this scale before? ___________

What type of scale is it? ______________________________

What happens to this scale in the last cluster chord? ______________________

Here's a helpful hint. Practice these cluster chords in short sections, but play them with the sound you want to hear right from the beginning. (If you combine details such as **articulation** and dynamics with the actual notes, it will take you less time to learn the complete piece.)

Use fifth-finger voicing on the RH chords to create a shimmering brilliance like moonlight reflected on the water.

Find the Tritones and the Major 7ths!

The intervals of a **tritone** and a major 7th have a strong effect on the sound colors of this piece.

Why do you think Louie has chosen these particular intervals?

____

What is a tritone? ______________________________

Play both intervals and listen to the sound. How would you describe them?

tritone: ______________________________

major 7th: ______________________________

See if you can find all the tritones and major 7ths in *O Moon*. Put a small mark in your score beside each one you identify.
(CLUE: Some of these intervals are tricky to find. Look for both **harmonic** and **melodic intervals**, and don't forget the grace notes!)

Keep experimenting with your sound, trying to communicate the atmosphere, the varying densities, and the shades of tonal color that describe the title.

Milonga del ángel

Astor Piazzolla (1921–1992)

Piano Repertoire 8 page 62

CD 8 / track 23

The Argentinian composer Astor Piazzolla lived in New York and Argentina, playing in films and dance bands, before achieving huge success in the 1950s and 1960s as a solo performer. By that time, he had won a government scholarship to study under the influential teacher Nadia Boulanger in Paris. She encouraged him as a composer to discover the possibilities of his own native music, and thus he turned his attention to the tango.

The vivacious style of Piazzolla's "nuevo tango" attracted a massive South American audience. In the 1970s, he returned to Paris because of political turmoil in Argentina. Piazzolla's international breakthrough came in the early 1980s with the formation of his Quinteto Tango Nuevo (violin, piano, guitar, and bass). Today, Piazzolla's music enjoys a wide audience thanks to its compelling fusion of folkloric beauty and contemporary tension.

Music and Dance of Argentina

Piazzolla played the *bandoneon* — an accordion operated entirely by buttons (that is, with no keyboard) invented in the 1840s by and named for Heinrich Band. The bandoneon is used in Argentinian popular music.

The *milonga* was a popular dance in the suburbs of Buenos Aires during the last decades of the 19th century. It is one of the most important sources (together with the *tango Andaluz* and the *habañera*) of the Argentine tango.

Rhythmic Style

The word "tango" refers both to the Argentine dance tango performed by couples, and to the genre of music played for that dance. The tango rhythm is based on **syncopated** patterns within a $\frac{2}{4}$ or $\frac{4}{4}$ meter.

Here are four syncopated rhythms from *Milonga del ángel.*

Tap each one, hands together, until the rhythm is secure. Then find all the places where that rhythm occurs in the music.

What do all four rhythms have in common?

____

(CLUE: Look at the third beat of the measure.)

This marking takes the stress from the second half of the measure and shifts it an eighth beat earlier, creating a syncopation that seems to defy gravity. Enjoy feeling suspended over the second half of the measure.

Play the RH melody alone from mm. 1–8. What do you notice? _______________

____

How do these notes sound once the changing LH harmonies are sounded against them?____

In mm. 10, 26, and 27, there are sixteenth figures, which need to blend smoothly into the melody line. What do they remind you of? _________________________

What do the subtle chords of mm. 17–20 remind you of in a dance band?______

____

Create your own Dance Band!

Explore the syncopated rhythm of *Milonga del ángel* further with your teacher or a friend. One person could play the melody separately, and the others could divide up the rhythm on either piano, or percussion, or guitar. If you have access to two pianos in the same room, have one person play the melody in octaves on one piano and the other person play the accompaniment on the second piano. The guitar can play the arpeggiated chords. Remember, you can beat out the rhythm on any surface!

Now look through the music for rhythms that involve triplets.

Copy each different one here, and indicate the rhythmic value of the triplet figure.

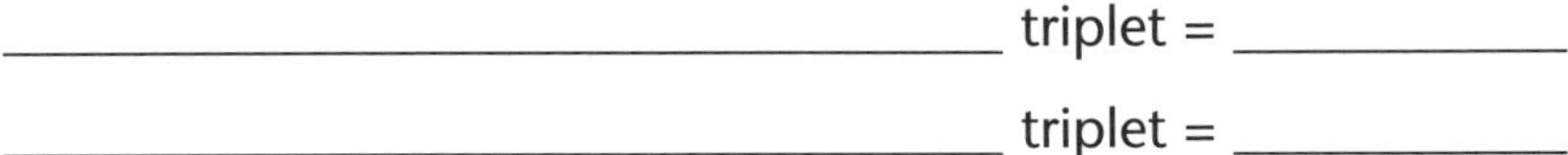

These rhythms, and others like them, suggest the skill and elegance of those who dance the tango.

A Contrasting Section

What is the key of *Milonga del ángel?* ___________

The middle section of this dance features a thicker chordal texture and richly **dissonant** harmonies.

Where does this section begin? ___________

What is the key of this section? ___________

How is this key related to the home key? ___________

Piazzolla uses specific intervals and repeated patterns to create a rich and intense musical statement. Here is the chord formed by the first RH and LH notes in m. 33.

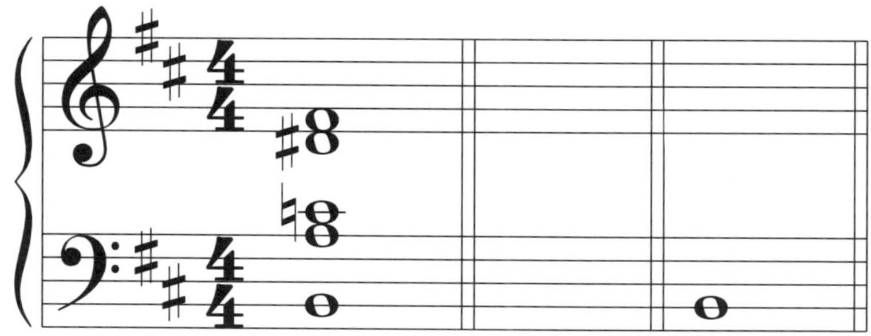

Extract a triad in root position from these notes, and write it in close position beside the chord. In the third space, write the bass note and the two remaining notes, and name the intervals formed between the bass note and each of these notes.

These intervals — especially the larger one — give an edge and sparkle to the harmony. To prove it, play m. 33 replacing all the C naturals with B, and then play it as written. Which version has more spice?

There are two patterns in mm. 33–44. The first one involves the LH rhythm.

Can you see a repeating rhythm here? How long is it, and how many times is it repeated? ____

Now look at the measures following this repeated rhythm. Can you spot a **sequence** in this passage?

How long is the pattern? ___________

Does it involve both hands? ___________

What is the interval between repetitions? Is this a falling or a rising sequence?

___________________ ___________________

As you learn this passage, listen for the expression of controlled passion that runs through it. If you enjoy it, your listeners certainly will!

Pink and **Crimson**

Robert Starer (1924–)

Piano Repertoire 8
page 65

CD 8 / tracks 24 & 25

Starer was born in Vienna in 1924, and became an American citizen in 1957. He received his musical education at the State Academy in Vienna, the Jerusalem Conservatoire, and the Juilliard School. Starer served on the faculty at Juilliard from 1949–1974 and was appointed professor of music at Brooklyn College, CUNY in 1963. Starer's music is characterised by his use of chromaticism, modality, and driving rhythms. His orchestral works have been performed by major orchestras in the United States and abroad. Starer has also composed for the stage, including three operas and several ballets.

Musical Colors

Starer's collection entitled *Sketches in Color* has become quite popular among young pianists. This collection is literally a rainbow of sound. Each of its seven pieces paints a vivid musical impression of a particular color through a range of modern musical idioms.

The concept of relating music to colors is not a new one.

Can you think of pieces you have played or heard with titles that refer to colors?

____

____

You may already have your own ideas about the character or "mood" of these colors, crimson and pink.

Make a list of the first five words or ideas that come to mind when you think of each of these colors:

Pink	**Crimson**

Keep these descriptions in mind as you explore Starer's musical concept of these two colors.

Pink — Cool Jazz

The **harmonic** style of this piece may remind you and your listeners of the spacious, lyrical quality of "cool jazz." Play mm. 1–4 hands together, then play each part alone.

___ ___ ___   ___ ___   ___ ___   ___ ___

This opening phrase seems to expand from one small motive in a spontaneous, expressive manner akin to **improvisation**.

How does Starer expand the rhythm of m. 1 in m. 2?

____

How do you react to this little motive as it gently unfolds? ____________________

The rhythmical movement also seems to unfold and increase in mm. 5–6 as Starer moves from 3 to before relaxing and receding in m. 7.

The double notes in the LH part expand up to the first beat of m. 3, and then contract.

Write the name of each LH interval on the example above.

Play this passage, and listen for the expansion to the openness of the climax of the phrase, followed by a gradual relaxation.

Shades of Pink

The theme of mm. 1–4 is repeated a number of times through the piece.

Where is the theme repeated a 3rd higher? ____________

What is the relation of the key in mm. 10–13 to that of mm. 1–4? ____________

Do you feel the new key has a "brighter" sound? ____________________

Rather than present straight repetitions of his melody, Starer repeats the triplet motive in m. 13 (**transposed** down an ____________ from m. 11) as a link between two statements.

What is surprising about the key introduced by the statement in mm. 14–17?

____

Is there any clue in the music that might suggest the shade of pink Starer has in mind at this point? ______________________________

Expressive Dissonance

Starer has used the **dissonance** of the smallest and largest intervals to explore greater expressivity. Let's take a closer look. The notes on the first beat of m. 1 (C, A, and G) create a dissonance. However, the G is an ***appoggiatura***, and the musical tension is relaxed when it **resolves**.

Which note does this *appoggiatura* resolve to? ___________

To fully appreciate the richness of the sound created in this measure, play m. 1 without the G (replace the G with an F).

Where is the other expressive *appoggiatura* in the LH part? ____________________

Look for other examples of expressive harmony created by *appoggiaturas* and **suspensions**.

Slow Jazz Rhythms

The frequent time signature changes also give this piece a relaxed, improvised quality. When you play these rhythms, keep an even quarter-note pulse, and resist the temptation to speed up in the shorter measures.

Play mm. 1–4 again, and this time, pay particular attention to the rhythm.

How does the change from $\frac{3}{4}$ to $\frac{2}{4}$ enhance the forward motion of the phrase? ________________________________

Crimson — The Whole is greater than its Parts

Crimson owes much of its effect to the skilful combination of simple but effective musical building blocks. Here are five excerpts from the music. Find each one, add the measure numbers to the excerpt, and play it. (You may find it helpful to play the adjacent measures as well so that you can hear the excerpt in its musical context.) Then match each excerpt to the description that best fits it, and answer the questions. The descriptions and questions are on p. 84.

Excerpt A
mm. ________

Excerpt B
mm. ________

f

Excerpt C
mm. ________

Excerpt D
mm. ________

Excerpt E
mm. ________

Excerpt ________

a final touch of humor — a simple cadence after all the excitement

What kind of cadence does Starer use? ___________

Excerpt ________

a melody in which the notes are all the same interval apart

What is the interval?___________

Excerpt ________

and Excerpt ________

two examples of broken triads

Identify the triads as major, minor, diminished, or augmented.

Excerpt _______: ________________________________

Excerpt _______: ________________________________

Excerpt ________

two driving *ostinato* figures — one in each hand

These figures clarify the subdivision of the 7/8 rhythm into a pattern of

_______ plus _______.

To practice this division of the meter, play scales with this accent pattern.

Why do you think this piece is called *Crimson*?

____

Comparing Colors

Starer's pair of pieces presents the perfect opportunity to showcase strong musical contrast. Place each term from the following mix under its appropriate title in the two columns below.

long, sustained sounds	unchanging meter	
fluid, flexible rhythms	gentle dynamic changes	dreamy and sentimental
sharp, jagged rhythmic outlines	changing meter	insistent and impetuous
violent dynamic contrasts	short sounds	

Pink	**Crimson**
______________	______________
______________	______________
______________	______________
______________	______________
______________	______________

How many of these descriptions correspond with the words you wrote about "pink" and "crimson" on p. 81?

Page d'album

Album Leaf

Claude Debussy (1862–1918)

Piano Repertoire 8 page 68

CD 8 / track 26

Debussy studied piano at the Paris Conservatory with Antoine Marmontel. After his graduation in 1880, he studied composition with Ernest Guiraud. In 1884 he won the Prix de Rome. Most of Debussy's works for piano expanded the expressive range of the instrument. The exotic musical colors, delicate layers of tone, and pedaling techniques produce effects comparable to those of the French Impressionistic painters. He was one of the most influential French composers his time, and his compositions had a profound effect on 20th-century music. Varying influences on his music — ranging from the ancient to the contemporary, and including the gamelan orchestra Debussy heard at the Paris Exposition of 1889 — resulted in an innovative and personal music language. His creative philosophy can be summarized by the final phrase of a poem by the French poet Charles Baudelaire entitled *Correspondances* — "ecstasy of the mind and senses."

This gentle waltz, originally titled *Pièce pour l'oeuvre du "Vêtement du blessé" (Pour le "vêtement" de ma petite mienne)* and dedicated to Emma Debussy, was composed in 1915. It was first presented at a wartime benefit concert on 24 March 1917 (one of several such concerts to which Debussy contributed), but was only published in 1933 under the title *Page d'album*.

A Simple Motive

This delicate miniature is a perfect introduction to the magic sensuality of Debussy's musical world as he spins an ever-changing panorama of colors and harmonies out of a simple melodic motive.

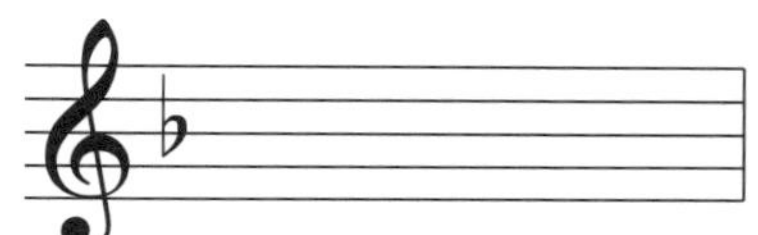

Write the notes of this motive as a 7th chord in root position. This chord contains a _______ triad and a _______ 7th.

List the measures where this motive is repeated exactly. mm. _______________
mm. _______________

Debussy also uses a **variation** of this motive as the continuation of the main melody. Write this motive here, and list the measures where it occurs.

mm. _______________

mm. _______________

mm. _______________

mm. _______________

mm. _______________

Broken Chords

Where does Debussy repeat these notes with a different rhythm? mm. ________

mm. ________

Compare how the changing lower texture affects the color of this motive.

____

How do you react to each? ______________________________

Where does Debussy use another descending arpeggiated 7th chord? mm. ________

mm. ________

Name the triad and the 7th in this chord. Is it the same as the 7th chord in the original motive? ____________________

In m. 13, Debussy expands the descending arpeggio to a 9th, and this in turn spins out into a shimmering broken-chord figure that continues until the original motive returns in m. 19. Play these measures and listen to the cumulative effect of these broken chords.

Can you write the notes of the broken chord in mm. 15–18 as a simple chord?

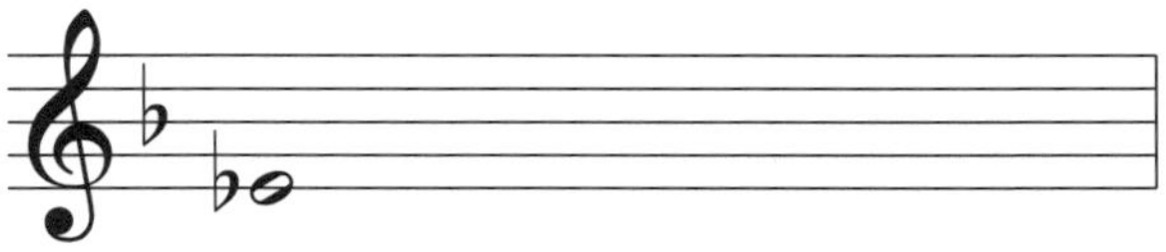

(CLUE: Don't attempt to write the notes in the order they are played. Start with E flat at the bottom, and fill in the other notes by 3rds. You will end up with a very tall chord!)

This chord is typical of Debussy's sound. Instead of expanding a chord by repeating notes in different octaves, he adds 3rds. The absence of a strong tonal pull in these harmonies gives the sound a quality of weightlessness.

An Oscillating Melody

Now play mm. 22–30, and listen to the contrasting texture of these measures. Here Debussy is working with several layers of sound.

In this passage, the melody moves back and forth among ___________ notes.

In mm. 22–26, the accompaniment shifts back and forth between two chords:

___________ and ___________.

In mm. 27–30, the harmony changes. The LH plays a ___________ chord with one note missing. The RH supplies the missing note along with another note.

The Final Moments

Play mm. 31–38, and compare the sound with that of mm. 1–4.

Write the LH chords in mm. 1–4 in root position.

1 – 4

Three of these chords are 7ths. What type of 7ths are they?

____

Name the fourth chord. ______________

Does Debussy use the same harmonies in mm. 31–38?

____

What new harmonies does he introduce?

____

____

How does Debussy stretch out the RH melody of mm. 1–4 to extend over eight measures? ______________

French Nuances

You may want to consult a French dictionary for the meaning of the terms that Debussy uses.

Modéré	______________
Cédez	______________
Mouv^{t} (Mouvement)	*a tempo*
En serrant	______________
En retenant	______________
un peu animé	______________
Très retenu	______________

The sum total of these many subtle changes of tempo, including ***rubato*** in mm. 27–30, is a fluid motion and delicate shading that is typical of Debussy's Impressionist style.

Mysterious Summer's Night

Larysa Kuzmenko (1956–)

Piano Repertoire 8
page 69

CD 8 / track 27

Kuzmenko was born in Toronto. She studied music at the University of Toronto and graduated with a degree in composition in 1979. As a pianist, Kuzmenko has given solo recitals and has also performed as a chamber musician. She teaches at The Royal Conservatory of Music. The list of her compositions includes a piano concerto and works for band, chamber ensemble, piano, and voice.

An Impression

What does the title *Mysterious Summer's Night* bring to your mind. . . night in the city, late evening in the country, gathering shadows, bright stars, sounds in the darkness. . .? Perhaps your interpretation of this music will bring these thoughts to your listeners as well. This charming, impressionistic piece is a good example of music that evokes a mood. It calls for a rich *cantabile* tone and a sensitive feeling for color.

Musical Breathing

Mysterious Summer's Night does not follow a regular pattern of phrases and **cadences**. The music is structured in one- or two-measure "gestures" that end with chords that provide a moment of rest. For example, when you play mm. 1–4, think of a short resting point after mm. 1 and 2, and a slightly longer one after m. 4. The melodies and harmonies indicate the resting points.

The rhythms are slow and simple, and many of the gestures begin on an upbeat. In the space below, write five different rhythmical patterns that function as upbeats.

Play mm. 1–4 again and describe the sensation of entering the phrase from each differing style of upbeat.

How do the variations affect movement, color or gravity? ____________________

____

____

____

____

Although the time signature of the music is $\frac{4}{4}$, you may find it helpful to count an easy pulse of two beats to the measure.

How will this slower meter affect the motion of the music?

____

Think of the slow, relaxed breathing pattern of someone who is resting.

An Harmonic Ebb and Flow

Although the music has a contemporary sound, it is based on traditional keys and harmonies. Kuzmenko uses a number of devices to enhance the sound. She uses **chromatic** notes and harmonies for color. Play the RH of mm. 5–7, then look at the notes.

If you write the notes in this passage in "scale" order, what type of scale would you have? _______________________

Where does Kuzmenko use these notes in a scale passage?

____

She uses 7th chords with altered notes or additional notes. Play m. 10.

Name the notes of the 7th chord in the first half of this measure.

____

(CLUE: There is an ***appoggiatura*** on the first beat.)

In this measure, Kuzmenko further obscures the identity of the 7th chord with a **cross relation**.

Which note appears in both natural and flattened forms?_______________

A Larger Structure

Many of the gestures seem to fall into groups of four measures.

Write and name the final chords of mm. 4, 8, 16, 20, and 24.

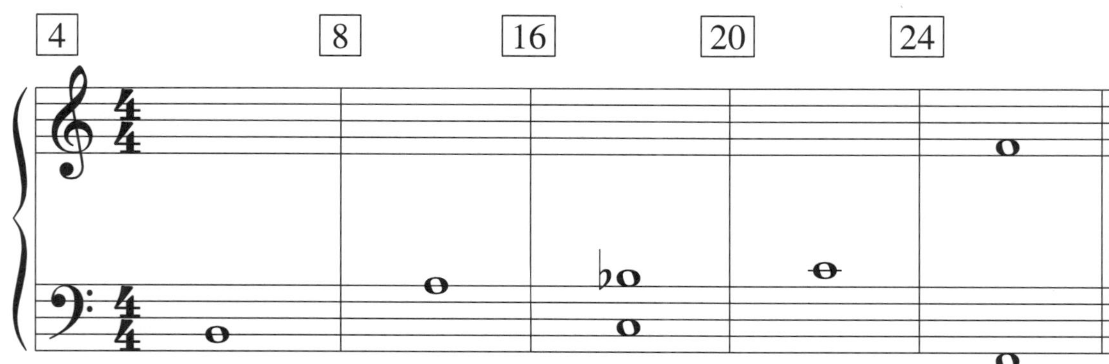

The music of *Mysterious Summer's Night* falls into three sections.

A	mm. 1–8
B	mm. 9–16
A_1	mm. 17–24

What is the key of the A section? ____________

How would you describe the character of this section?________________________

Does the B section present a contrasting character? How would you describe it?

____

What markings does Kuzmenko use to enhance the contrasting character?

____

This section is highly chromatic but seems to suggest C as the **dominant** of F minor.

The section ends with a cadence in mm. 16–17.

Name the type of cadence and the two chords.

____

____

(CLUE: The third of the second chord is in the RH melody.)

What is the key of the A_1 section? _________________________

The Pedal

This piece is marked *con pedale*, and the pedal will help you to keep a *legato* line through notes you cannot connect with your fingers, but make sure the harmonies are always clear and the melody is not blurred. As a general rule, change the pedal twice per measure in this piece. Listen to the sound and find the exceptions to this rule.

How many times will you change the pedal in m. 14?

____

In mm. 5–7, experiment with light pedaling. This may help you to connect the LH position changes smoothly.

The Gentle Waltz

Oscar Peterson (1925–)

Piano Repertoire 8
page 70

CD 8 / track 28

Montreal-born Oscar Peterson is one of Canada's most celebrated jazz musicians. He is renowned for his impeccable piano technique, his highly original compositions, and the unending variety and brilliance of his improvisation. In his early years, he was influenced by such legendary jazz musicians as Nat King Cole and Art Tatum, but he quickly developed his own musical identity, to such an extent that he was attracting attention across North America while still in his teens. Peterson's compositions show influences as diverse as blues, gospel, modern jazz, and Canadian folk music.

The Gentle Waltz is an excellent introduction to the rich and sophisticated **harmonic** language of modern jazz, which uses added tones called extensions (9ths, 11ths, and 13ths as well as the familiar 7ths) combined with classical features such as **sequences** and ***appoggiaturas***.

Jazz Extensions

One way of expanding the triads on which traditional harmony is based is to add 3ds to the chord to make 7ths, 9ths, 11ths, and even 13ths above their root. To get a sense of the sound of these chords, try this experiment.

Write a C major triad above the C of this scale.

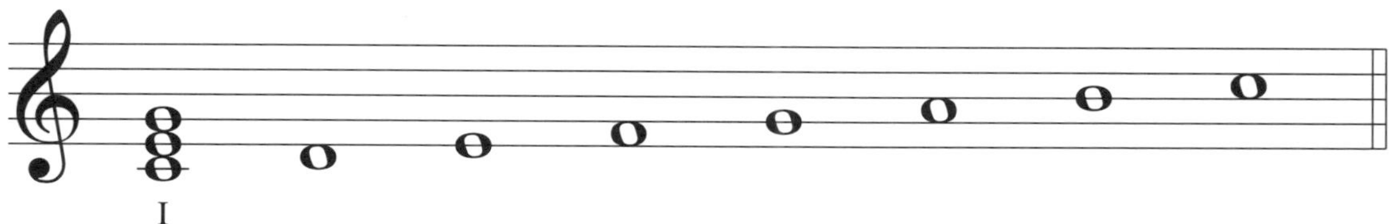

Add a 7th above the root, play the chord, and listen to the sound.

Now write a 7th chord above each note of the C major scale. (Use the notes of the C major scale — don't add any accidentals.) Label the chords I^7, II^7, etc. Play this scale and listen to the sound.

Play your 7th scale in different registers, and experiment with adding octaves in the LH. If this seems too easy, **transpose** the scale to two other major keys! Now try the same experiment with other added tones. Add a 9th (again, above the root of each chord), play the chord, and listen to the sound. This will give you a small taste of the harmonic palette Peterson uses in *The Gentle Waltz*.

A Note on Extended Harmony

When properly voiced, one or more notes will be omitted from an extended chord. For example, the 3rd is usually omitted from a dominant 11th chord to avoid the **dissonance** created by the 11th.

Chord extensions can be **chromatically** altered: 9ths can be raised or lowered, 11ths can be raised, and 13ths can be lowered. Chord symbols will also be affected. This piece contains many minor 7th chords with a lowered 5th, and many dominant 7th chords with both diatonic and lowered 9ths. (When a minor 7th chord has a lowered 5th, the chord becomes a half-diminished 7th chord.)

Exploring Oscar Peterson's Harmony

Now let's have a look at *The Gentle Waltz*. Play the first phrase and listen particularly to the chords. Now look at m. 1.

Which chord in your 7th scale matches the notes in this measure, with the exception of one accidental? ii7

Add the accidental to your chord, and circle it.

Can you find the notes of one of your chords in m. 2? G V7
(CLUE: The root is the bass note.)

This chord isn't a 7th chord — it's a 9th chord. (The A flat is a 9th above the bass note.)

How can you explain the E on the first beat?
+7 above the F
(CLUE: This note resolves to D. Think of an Italian term that suggests "leaning.")

Add the A flat to the chord in your scale and change the label to indicate that it is a 9th chord.

Which of your 7th chords matches most of the notes in m. 3?
iii7

In this case, the notes that don't fit your chord are **non-chord tones** — that is, extra notes that don't belong to the harmony but have been added to enhance the texture.

Does the back-and-forth motion of these chords look like a slower version of an **ornament** you might see in Baroque music? What is the name of the ornament?
turn (mordent)
(CLUE: Check the descriptions of ornaments in the Glossary at the back of this *Workbook*.)

These three measures you have just explored will give you an idea of the structure of Peterson's harmony and melody. Try doing the same kind of exploration with other passages.

Clues to Interpretation

When you play the melody only, listen to its arched shape. You will need to give it many more subtle dynamic shadings than can be accurately notated. Experiment with shaping this melody, and make sure the single notes ring out above the chords, even at a *pianissimo* level!

Take note of the tempo indication.

What does "almost hesitantly" suggest to you about the mood or character of this waltz? ______

Think of ways in which this opening indication might guide your musical feeling.

Do you wish your performance to sound carefully planned and structured – or a little as though you are **improvising** it on the spot? ______

Sequences

Sequences are used extensively in some jazz styles. In chromatic passages they may be hard to spot on paper. Your ear will be your best guide, and the bass line will also give you a clue.

There is a sequence in the middle section of *The Gentle Waltz*. Where is it?

____

How long is the pattern, and what is the **interval** distance between the repetitions? ____________________________

Make Your Own Music

Each measure of this passage is based on a 7th chord. Write these chords above the bass notes on the staff.

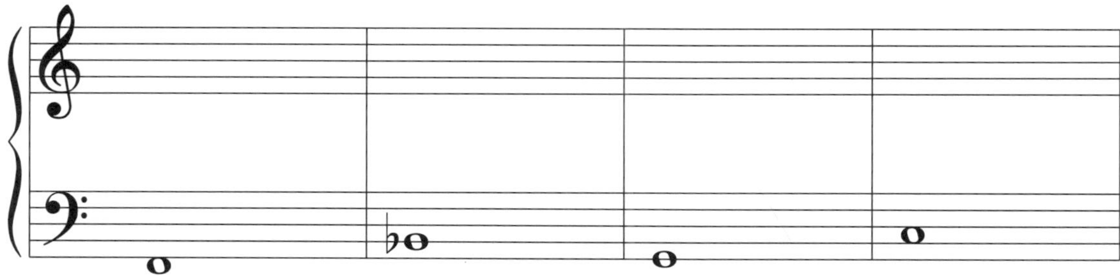

Now's your chance to have fun. Use this sequence of 7th chords as a basis for an improvisation. Stick to the notes of the 7th chords until you are familiar with the **chord progression**. Once the basic notes are secure, see where these harmonies lead you. Experiment with different melodies, and change the chords around. You can either extend the sequence for a few more measures, or create your own ending for the phrase.

Performing Jazz

You have just been experimenting with improvisation. Much of jazz is improvised in the same manner — working from a basis such as a melody or a chord progression. *The Gentle Waltz*, however, is not improvised. It is written down — complete with dynamic and **articulation** markings. The secret to performing written jazz is to make it sound like an improvisation rather than a straight "reading." When you play music from earlier periods, you give it your own personal interpretation. When you play *The Gentle Waltz*, you follow Peterson's written score, but you also give the music your personal interpretation. This is a creative process that happens each time you play the piece — and in this way, it is an improvisation.

accidental a sharp, flat, or natural sign in front of a note. An accidental affects a note for only one measure; it is cancelled by a bar line.

Alberti bass a keyboard accompaniment pattern consisting of broken chords, named after Dominico Alberti (1710–*ca* 1740)

appoggiatura a **non-chord tone** played on a strong beat

articulation the way in which notes are played: long or short, separated (detached, *staccato*) or joined together (*legato*)

binary form a structure of two sections (AB), both of which may be repeated. In **rounded binary form**, the B section ends with a partial repeat of A.

bridge a connecting passage

cadence two or more chords in succession that conclude a section or composition:

perfect (authentic) cadence: V–I

imperfect (half) cadence: I–V or IV–V

deceptive cadence: V–VI

plagal cadence: IV–I

cantabile in a singing style

character piece a 19th-century miniature for piano depicting a scene or mood

chord three or more notes sounding together; a **chord progression** is a series of chords

chromatic use of notes ouside of, or in addition to, the usual degrees of a major or minor scale

circle of 5ths the circular, clockwise arrangement of the 12 keys in an order of ascending 5ths (C, G, D, etc.)

cluster chord (tone cluster) a highly dissonant, closely spaced collection of pitches sounded simultaneously

coda a concluding section added to the basic form. (In Italian, *coda* means "tail.") A **codetta** is a concluding passage added to the end of a theme.

consonance notes sounding together that produce a relatively pleasing and stable sound

counterpoint see contrapuntal texture

cross relation (false relation) the succession of a pitch in one voice by a chromatic alteration of that pitch in another voice

Da Capo al Fine from the beginning to the *fine* (end)

degrees of the scale

- I tonic
- II supertonic
- III mediant
- IV subdominant
- V dominant
- VI submediant
- VII leading tone

diminished 7th chord a chord consisting of a diminished triad with a diminished 7th added above the root

dissonance notes sounding together that produce a relatively harsh or discordant sound requiring **resolution** to a **consonance**

dominant 7th chord a chord consisting of the dominant triad with a minor 7th added above the root

drone long, sustained notes, usually in the bass part

enharmonic tones of the same pitch spelled differently (e.g., C sharp and D flat are enharmonic equivalents)

fermata a pause

grace note note played before the beat; printed in small type and usually slurred to the note it ornaments

harmony parts or voices sounding together; **implied harmony** is the harmonic progression implied by the notes of a melody

hemiola the proportion of two to three – a change in rhythm where two measures of triple time are made to sound like three measures or duple time, or vice versa

imitation exact repetition of one part or voice in another pitch, voice or section; non-exact repetition is called **free imitation**

improvisation the art of creating music spontaneously as it is being performed

interval the distance between two notes harmonic interval – an interval consisting of two *simultaneous* tones

melodic interval – an interval consisting of two *consecutive* tones

inversion the reversal of a pattern or interval (turning upside-down, mirror image)

legato smoothly

mode a type of scale that gives a special flavor to music. Modes are the basis for much church music, folk music, and jazz. Some modes are:

Aeolian: white notes from A to A

Ionian: white notes from C to C

Dorian: white notes from D to D

Phrygian: white notes from E to E

Lydian: white notes from F to F

modulation a change of key

mordent an **ornament** consisting of the alternation of the written notes and the note below

motive a small unit or figure, either melodic or rhythmic

non-chord tone a note foreign to the chord but sounded at the same time as the chord

ornament note, or notes, added to a melody for decoration. Ornaments include mordent, turn, trill

ostinato a persistently repeated motive or phrase

parallel motion movement in the same direction where the interval between the two voices remains the same

passing note a **non-chord tone** that connects two consonant pitches by stepwise motion

pedal point a long, held note, usually in the bass, which is sustained while harmonies change in the other parts

phrase a short passage, often of two to four measures

portato halfway between *staccato* and *legato*

resolution a progression from **dissonance** to **consonance**

rubato an elastic, flexible tempo using slight variations of speed to enhance musical expression

sequence repetition of a motive at a different pitch

slur a small group of notes under a curved line which is played *legato*

sonata (sonatina) a work for one or more solo instruments, usually in several movements. A sonatina is a little sonata.

sonata form form of an extended movement of a sonata, with three main sections:

exposition, in which two keys are contrasted with each other, often by means of separate, contrasting themes

development, in which musical material from the exposition is varied and reworked

recapitulation, in which the themes from the exposition are restated in the tonic key

staccato very short

suspension a non-chord tone held over from the previous beat

syncopation a shifting of the normal beat or accent, resulting in an emphasis on the weak beat

tempo rate of speed or pace of music:

a tempo (Tempo I) return to the previous tempo

accelerando getting faster

allegretto not as fast as *allegro*

allegro fast, "cheerful"

allegro ma non trappo quickly but not too quickly

andante moderately slow or walking pace

andantino slower than *andante*

lento slow

poco più mosso a little more motion

presto very fast

rallentando (rall.) slowing down

ritardando (rit.) slowing down

ritenuto (riten.) slowing down suddenly

*sforzando (**sfz**)* strongly accented

tenuto hold a note for its full value

ternary form a structure of three sections (ABA) in which B is a contrast to A. The repeat of A can be a little different.

texture the interweaving of melodic and harmonic elements in the musical fabric

hemophonic texture — a principal melody with accompanying harmony

contrapuntal texture — combining several melodic lines

Tierce de Picardie a major chord at the end of a piece in a minor key

transposition playing or writing music in a key that is different from the original

trill an **ornament** that turns around the principal note

tritone augmented 4th or dimished 5th

turn an ornament that turns around the principal note

variation a repetition of a motive or theme with changes — the changes can be slight or significaant